New Paradigm Psychology

Embracing the New: Putting the Heart into Counseling and Psychology Practice

T0096991

New Paradigm Psychology

Embracing the New: Putting the Heart into
Counseling and Psychology Practice

Claudia Vayda

**PSYCHE
BOOKS**

Winchester, UK
Washington, USA

First published by Psyche Books, 2018
Psyche Books is an imprint of John Hunt Publishing Ltd., No. 3 East Street, Alresford
Hampshire SO24 9EE, UK
office1@jhpbooks.net
www.johnhuntpublishing.com
www.psyche-books.com

For distributor details and how to order please visit the 'Ordering' section on our website.

Text copyright: Claudia Vayda 2017

ISBN: 978 1 78099 811 4
978 1 78279 908 5 (ebook)
Library of Congress Control Number: 2017942028

A CIP catalogue record for this book is available from the British Library.

Design: Stuart Davies

Printed and bound by CPI Group (UK) Ltd, Croydon, CR0 4YY, UK

We operate a distinctive and ethical publishing philosophy in
all areas of our business, from our global network of authors to
production and worldwide distribution.

Contents

Foreword

When Claudia and I met over 10 years ago at a self development intensive, our affinity was instant. We shared a mutual respect for the therapeutic space and the importance of bringing our most authentic and truest selves to clients. Connecting with a fellow counsellor who was aware of and acknowledged the existence of 'energy', its influence, and importance within the therapeutic relationship, gave us much to talk about. We felt like 'therapeutic kin'. This was the first time I had met someone who I felt truly understood why I chose to be a counsellor. We shared many self development intensives in the years to follow.

With this book, Claudia has opened the window to allow a refreshing breeze to flow into the therapeutic space. The use of 'energy' language is not new where terms such as psychic energy, mental energy, instinct energy and psychological energy are all commonplace. We know that we sense how others feel and can even respond in ways others want us to without uttering a single word – we feel it. The trick is to ensure our use of this energy and response to it in others is for upliftment, growth with an absent of judgment, control, limit or condition. This is wisdom in practice.

Claudia's years working in private practice and in schools as a heart centred counsellor has allowed her the experience and expertise to write this guidebook for therapists. She challenges readers to go deeper than 'self development' modules allow, connecting with a deep knowing sense within. Sometimes confronting beliefs born from academic study is enough to prepare therapists to work with clients, while introducing ways that 'inner' growth and evolvement contributes to the therapeutic relationship in ways that no-one talks about. Claudia's book says it is time we opened our minds and hearts to accept the influence of our presence and talk about it. Heart centred therapy for human relationships is the 'let us' rather than 'I know' approach to healing and connection.

I wonder what it would be like if we consciously chose to bring the best to and out of one another regardless of what was occurring intra-psychically, and live as an example of potential, hope, compassion and love. We know love is the greatest healer of all in its many qualities, and has many expressions such as kindness, nurture, compassion, space, care, thoughtfulness, encouragement, gratitude, appreciation, connection. Claudia and I both live this way of self accountability and growth; we bring it to one another and to each of our clients. We know it feels different and has greatly assisted our clients in ways that have, up until now, been difficult to articulate. Claudia puts words to the feelings.

This book is about awareness primarily, and accountability secondly. Therapists cannot be neutral; they bring themselves, their resolved stuff, their unresolved stuff, their triggers, feelings and all that they are to every session. What makes this book timely and worthwhile is its focus of listening with the heart rather than the mind, to feel something different amongst the words and pages, and to actually apply it to oneself. Be prepared to be confronted, challenged and consciously choose to open – just the very thing we encourage our clients to do – and by being a living example we naturally encourage others to be the same.

Linda Koen
Holistic Counsellor

Foreword

Claudia has written a very original work for mental health practitioners to rethink and reinvent how and why they do therapy.

She gives refreshing examples of reframing the relationship in counselling and the importance of cultivating psycho-spiritual principles such as compassion, curiosity and hope.

Claudia moves the work of counselling to a larger context and explores the need to forge a larger perspective of healing, and one that incorporates a healthier impact on the environment.

She does this skilfully by invoking energy and presence in the healing process and by clarifying the necessity of developing being over doing.

Her work utilises the contemporary practices of positive psychology and self-determination which move counselling from a deficit focus to strength-building.

The book breathes new life into the counselling relationship allowing for heart-based conversation guided by compassionate awareness and empathy. Accordingly, room is made available for spontaneity and creativity.

Her new paradigm is hopeful for clients and society and respectful of the healing process.

Claudia has worked hard in her personal life to live by these practices and principles and has also used this experience to create a compassionate approach to therapy that embraces the whole person as well as bringing forth those wonderful qualities of joy , love and healing.

Dr Steve Zolezzi, Psychologist

Acknowledgements

I would like to express my deepest gratitude to all those below for their contributions to the creation of this book, and for their friendship. Thank you all so much.

To Michael and Segolene King for the inspiration to write, and their unwavering support and love over the lengthy process that it turned out to be.

To Linda Koen, my dear friend and fellow traveller for her encouragement, ideas, and for showing me what 'embracing the new' really looks like.

To Jenna Cornell and Julie Skinner, the early readers of my manuscript for their feedback and suggestions.

To my brother Toby Burrows for his generosity.

To Steve Zolezzi for his input and contagious enthusiasm.

Introduction

Therapy is an ever-changing field to work in. It is the constantly moving, living breathing ebb and flow of relationship, emotional interaction and energetic connection. It is the exploration of the messiness and complexity of humanness.

It's very hard for us to tell objectively how effective we are, how well we do our job. Therapy moves in fits and starts, quickly, slowly and sometimes seemingly backwards. In fact, all therapists show some level of faith, trust and hope, just to stay in the job. We have to trust that our work is effective and having some impact for the benefit of the client. Of course we have visible and obvious 'successes' — and, indeed, 'failures' — but with other clients it can often be hard to tell, and sometimes the benefits of the work we do with people flower long after therapy has ended, and we are no longer in contact.

I think it is because of this difficulty in quantifying what we do, that therapists are some of the hungriest professionals I have come across for professional development, books and conferences, always wanting new learning and skills to integrate and to add to their 'tool box.'

I aim to keep this book readably short — I know how much you all have to read! — and to really focus on some simple concepts and processes that are equally beneficial to the treatment of clients in therapy, and to our own self care as counselors and therapists. This is not a new treatment approach, but simply an exploration of how to enhance both the therapist and clients' experience of therapy, to get better results and to move the act and idea of therapy into much more of its potential as a healing, nurturing and growth encouraging practice. It is also applicable to far more than simply the therapy hour. It is in fact relevant to a whole lifestyle change for us, as therapists, to enable us to live as much of our own potential as possible, as well as being able to assist others to reach theirs. This book is a reminder that in order to be the most effective therapist and psychologist we can be we must see our work as fully in alignment with how we live our lives. It is possible to get a good outcome working with a client, when we do not walk the talk of what we teach, but we will never get the best outcome that way, neither for ourselves nor for those who consult us.

In this book I will be addressing issues, such as holding a space for clients, and minding our own energy, as well as noticing what other people's energy does to us and how to address this. I will be delving at times into the 'spiritual' field, but bear with me! When we work with people we all come to understand that there is more to what is going on than a simple chemical imbalance or a lack of resilience, important though these are. The question is why, and how to assist, and we have to move further into areas that aren't typically psychological to address these issues. This is not new, in fact the frontiers of what is relevant to, and interesting for, psychologists are constantly being pushed out, and spirituality has already well and truly been introduced into the literature of psychology. I aim here to explore just a bit further, and discover what could be helpful to us as practitioners.

Over and over therapists write books that make the obligatory nod to their preferred treatment style, involving tools-skills and techniques. However, the largest portion of this particular book is about the relationship, the sense of safety and support for the client, and the miracles that happen that we cannot really explain. These miracles occur only when there is love and compassion in a judgment free zone.

Essentially we are no different from our clients, and are walking the same path on this complicated human journey. The practices and disciplines outlined in this book, and indeed the ideas discussed and expounded here are as relevant for use on the self of the practitioner as they are for use with clients. I would go even so far as to say that unless you submit to the discipline of these practices and make the commitment to be the best you can be, then you will not be able to use these ideas to any useful degree. This is not a book that tells you how to fix people. It operates on the ancient axiom, "Physician heal thyself." All then flows from here. The greater your clarity, understanding, compassion and awareness, the more you can be of service to other souls walking this path. Welcome to the beginning of the journey.

Chapter 1

The changing role of psychologists: choosing your path

Knowing yourself is the beginning of all wisdom. Aristotle

As I read journal and books, attend conferences and speak with colleagues, I have started to wonder what is happening in counseling psychology. There seems to be a widening split, almost a crisis of identity. On the one hand there is such a huge and burgeoning interest in the interface of spiritual ideas and psychology. The exploration of the place of such things as compassion, altruism, gratitude, love and joy in the happiness and the mental, emotional and physical health of the human being is enjoying much attention from a wide variety of scientists, researchers, spiritual leaders and those in practice in the helping professions, such as psychologists, counselors therapists and doctors.

On the other hand we have the increased scientificization (yes, I have made this word up) of psychology. As psychology has become more regulated, and more mainstream, we have developed a far more pathology focused and medical-like attitude and approach to our work. There is a push for evidence based therapies that can be manualized and even administered by computer, a focus on pathology and diagnosis, and a lessened interest in creating relationship and coming from the heart in therapy.

So where are we going, and how can we reconcile these two seemingly opposite ways of being? It seems to me that the way it is going suggests that we can choose from a couple of paths. The path I and many others are choosing is the path from the heart. The true work of exploring what it means to be human with our clients, not so that they can be happy, or live perfect lives or be free from emotional pain, but so that they, and we, can experience, learn grow, and develop. It's about making room in our lives to wonder, experience, and find joy, even in the midst of difficulty and pain.

Coming from the heart honors the humanness of our relationships with our clients and truly puts us alongside rather than in a one-up position. We are sharing the journey.

This book is for those of us who feel called to a different work, a new way. It is for those who would like to work as therapists and counselors with all kinds of people, and to be able to help facilitate their growth and movement emotionally, mentally and spiritually.

Psychology as a profession is changing under our eyes. What once was considered quite an alternative and even controversial field has now become so mainstream it is even covered by Medicare. There are psychologists in every school and every corporation. The roles of psychologists are ever widening, and there are now many different types of psychologists all requiring different training. Counseling psychology, and therapy, is my interest and focus here, and it also is changing, with so many different counseling approaches, techniques and schools of thought. As psychology changes, we as psychologists and counselors need to start deciding what it is we want it to become, so we can direct the changes and not be dictated to by government, or insurance companies.

I see that we are entering a new era in psychology, so let us take the opportunity now to decide what that will look like. We need to be ready for this next challenge and start working now on what we want to see. I can see psychology, if we allow it, take a role in nurturing, developing and healing, trailblazing a new way and taking a place among the teachers and healers in the new world.

I see the aims of psychology to be for a psychologically

healthy society; to promote and focus on health, rather than disease. To move towards an individual approach for clients or perhaps to simply understand that all are on their unique, but of course similarly human, journey. To move away from the paradigm of normal, of right and wrong ways to feel, of fixing those who don't fit in; to be the forerunners in the development of self-empowerment, and human spiritual growth in humanity. To allow our understanding of humanness to be a resource for humanity as it grows, learns and develops.

Wouldn't it be wonderful if people could, and did, see a psychologist or therapist preventatively, as is becoming more common in both traditional and complementary medicine? Imagine having clients who wished to come in to maintain and even further strengthen their mental/emotional health, their resilience, happiness, contentedness and self-worth; having clients who are looking for a positive outcome, a reaching higher towards their potential, rather than simply looking for the amelioration of symptoms. This would be such a wonderful way to work, with motivated and healthy people who wish to go just that bit further, to meet more of their potential. We know, as professionals, that there is always more work to be done—on ourselves, as well as with our clients. There is always further to go if a client wishes it. It seems, though, that as we medicalize psychology we run the risk of losing these 'healthy' clients, they simply see us as not for them, that they don't have enough pathology to warrant coming to see us. We are now seeing an increased interest in areas such as coaching and mentoring, and perhaps this is why, so as to be able to offer 'healthy' people an opportunity for growth and development, where they do not feel they have to be mentally ill. It would be a pity for Psychologists to lose this group, though, as we have the skills and training to work strongly and effectively in helping people be the best they can be. I am concerned that as we continue the trend of medicalizing psychology we end up with a counseling field split into fragments. As we start to call what we do 'psychological treatment', rather than 'therapy' or even 'counseling', we start to lose a cherished part of our role. Treatment implies fixing something that is wrong, sick or diseased, and so it limits the kinds of clients we attract and so the kind of work we do. This means some of what we could be doing is lost, and so other models are created to meet the needs of those who wish to do more and be more, but are not 'sick.' Coaching would be an example of that. The idea of coaching in this context had to be created in order to encourage those 'healthy' people to access more of their own potential.

I am not suggesting that psychologists do not work with the mentally ill, I understand that for many of us this is a critical and important part of our work, and rightly so. I am simply suggesting that this should not be the limit of our work, and particularly not be seen as the only useful work there is to be done. In trying to help people be able to fit in to society we can forget to look at society and wonder how it can be changed and influenced for the better, and where our role could be in this change. There is so much opportunity for positive work to be done with 'ordinary' people, in their quest to become extraordinary, helping them overcome their own self-imposed conditions and limitations, and so to help facilitate a critical mass of people who are enlightened, compassionate, loving and joyful, to help lead the way into a hopeful golden age for humanity.

This privileged profession could be one whose raison d'etre is to help all who wish it, to be the best they can be, and to know they can keep growing and developing. I would like to see psychotherapy as one of the professions that helps humanity as a whole move into the future, enabling people to know themselves better and more, and to keep moving towards an ideal. A profession that is able to provide people with tools to do the work themselves as well as facilitating this work as professionals. How high do we want to aim as the human race? Is this, what we have now, good enough? Can we be better, or should we simply be happy with not being ill? What more can we, as humans, strive and aim for, and what can we, as psychologists, do to help this process?

Though supporting those with mental illness and other issues to take part in a meaningful way in society is a large and essential part of a psychologists work, I think it is important that we do not discount the possibility of using our skills and knowledge to help advance humanity as a whole into the future. To be able also to facilitate those with the most potential to be their best and meet their potential in the same way as we do with those who are identified as needing help. We have such skill as a profession, and there is such potential in what we can do, and the role we can play in supporting human development could be so important. We must guard against limiting our vision, and at risk of sounding naïve, I think it is important that we revisit why we chose this 'helping' profession, and what we hoped it could be. That is the real possibility. That is the potential we could grow towards.

Let's take ownership of our profession and allow it to be what it could be—positive, facilitating, growthful and inspirational, taking a leading role in the mental, emotional and spiritual development of humanity as it moves into its future.

Questions to ponder

Sit with these questions over the next days and weeks and as you review your practice. What comes up can be transformative.

Who are we, as Psychologists/Therapists, and what is our job?

Is being a Psychologist/Therapist what you want it to be?

Is your current practice in line with why you became a Psychologist and/or a Therapist?

When you chose this path, what was your aim? Is it being fulfilled?

What would you like to change?

Where do you see psychology and/or Therapy in 100 years' time? 500 years' time?

Where would you like to see it?

Are these different? If so, how do we change that trajectory?

Chapter 2

Embracing the new: a new paradigm

With realization of one's own potential and self-confidence in one's ability one can build a better world.
Dalai Lama

We really have entered a new era. There is so much exploration and a blossoming in intellectual and scientific circles of new ideas and openness to the spiritual; discussion of the possibility of the existence of things that cannot be proven—yet. The excitement and optimism in the world of psychology and the worlds with which it collides is opening up whole new fields of research and fertile discussion, an openness of minds. Scientists can now explain, or at least start to research, things that previously would have been seen as unexplainable, such as how energy works, how feeling compassion affects our brain and happiness, and the fields of quantum physics and quantum mechanics, and how these micro-worlds relate to us, and give us the basis for fertile new discussions on energetic interactions.

What does it actually mean to be psychologically healthy? Being psychologically healthy is far more than the absence of mental disease, or fitting within the norms of the population. Psychological health is a positive state—not simply an absence of illness. It is where one is able to meet, or strive to meet, their potential, to overcome fear, doubt and disbelief, those things that limit us and prevent our growth. It is where we are able to take risks, as our self-worth is adequate to enable us to fail without losing ourselves, and our identity.

Usually clients seek us out when they have symptoms that are intruding upon their life in an unpleasant way, and that are impossible to ignore. Perhaps they find no pleasure in

14

anything, they are always exhausted, or they have panic attacks or compulsions. Perhaps they are suicidal, or feel completely alone in the world, or their relationships with partner, parents, children, friends or family are falling apart. Mostly these symptoms are seen as the illness. The client believes that if they can just get rid of their complaint all will be well again. It is important to remember though that these symptoms are simply that, symptoms. When they are present, there is always an underlying illness that may have been symptom-free for years. M. Scott Peck, in his book *The Road Less Travelled,* discusses this point and suggests that symptoms may be a wonderful opportunity for healing. Symptoms are a clue for us that things aren't going well, and Peck sees them as the beginning of the cure. Avoiding pain is avoiding growth, and indeed the pain that accompanies the symptoms creates the impetus for change.

True psychological health enables us to learn from our mistakes, and importantly, to be able to forgive ourselves for them. If we could see our mistakes and our messiness as simply an opportunity for growth and learning, so much of the angst, worry and self-hatred we see and feel would be gone. Instead we would simply feel gratitude, joy and trust that we are on the right path, on our own journey, and exactly where we need to be. Wow, what a difference! This is a world that I would like to see exist, and it does, sometimes, and with some people. Imagine if we all felt this. If we could all feel as we feel without judgment.

Where would counseling and psychology fit in this world? Where would they fit in a world that was psychologically healthy? Indeed, some would ask would they fit at all. I believe they would, and that the opportunities then for the profession to really contribute to the betterment of humanity would be magnified a thousandfold.

A world of love and acceptance is the kind of world we need to create to be able to take the next steps to true mental, emotional and spiritual well-being. Psychological health and clarity play a large part in this well-being. Growth, and the desire for it, must be honored and all our experience recognized for the gift it is, an aid to our learning and development.

There are no mistakes, just opportunities for learning and growth. This, however, is NOT an excuse for not striving, but an acceptance of reality, and a knowledge that we are all striving for the same thing. We mostly live at the moment within our separateness; even when we feel a sense of belonging it is often only in relation to the exclusion of some other group, such as in politics, in religion, in sport, in race or country of origin. We live in a world of 'us and them'. Imagine unity. Imagine knowing that all beings are looking for the same thing, are striving for the same thing. The level of compassion that this would engender in all of us would certainly change something!

As Einstein says in a famous quote:

A human being is a part of the whole, called by us the 'Universe', a part limited in time and space. He experiences himself, his thoughts and feelings, as something separate from the rest—a kind of optical delusion of his consciousness. This delusion is a kind of prison for us, restricting us to our personal desires and to affection for a few persons nearest to us. Our task must be to free ourselves from this prison by widening our circle of compassion to embrace all living creatures and the whole of nature in its beauty. Nobody is able to achieve this completely, but the striving for such achievement is in itself a part of the liberation and a foundation for inner security.

Our sense of separation is a delusion. Unity is the truth.

Harmony and unity

Being in harmony and unity allows us to let go of judgment on ourselves and others. We feel then a sense of belonging, and of oneness. It is separation that causes so much of the modern day distress we see daily. It is no coincidence that psychologists, therapists and counselors are becoming more and more mainstream, and that the DSM is getting bigger with every edition. We are becoming increasingly unhappy with our lives and our relationships, while at the same time expecting that we 'should' be happy all the time or at least most of it. We reason with ourselves that we should be feeling differently. We can't put our finger on why we should be so angry/grumpy/sad/flat/numb/miserable/despairing. We try and talk ourselves out of it, and in the process we make ourselves feel worse, because it doesn't work.

Research has shown that the most affluent societies are the unhappiest, and one of the most cited reasons for this is the apparent loss of community and relationships we find in wealthier consumer societies. We have become more separate from others. These days it is not just the sense of separation from those unlike us, such as other races, or even other towns as there was in the past. In our society this sense of separation has even spread to within our towns, workplaces and families. We have lost, in our size, the sense of social connectedness that previously existed; in its place is a sense of aloneness and separation for many of us. When we feel this separation we fail to see how all our actions and lives are intertwined. We fail to understand that we are all interdependent, that we all have our own particular purpose that fits beautifully in with all other particular purposes and that the world would be essentially different without even one of us in it. This sense of interdependence allows us to feel purpose, belonging and oneness. Then, we have a meaning.

Self-determination

Alongside that interdependence, self-determination can exist. The ability to take the courage to direct our own lives, make our own decisions and take responsibility for the consequences. This is an outrageous step, but the only way we can truly flourish and develop. We learn trust in ourselves, and we learn how to listen to our heart's direction. Most of us follow others, at least to some degree; we usually look for advice, at least in some matters, and we want approval from people we admire. When we lose the connection with our inner drive and purpose, we can use external sources to help us decide where we are going, and how to get there. Usually these sources are social norms, or the people in our lives and their approval or disapproval. We all would have had experiences where we felt it to be right to do something and got talked out of it. We lost our self-determination and gave into the fear of doing the wrong thing, we allowed ourselves to get talked into something different. Remember the feeling at this time? The sense of deflation, felt even through the satisfaction that we have chosen the 'right' thing, at least according to others. This leads to the risk that we feel our choices then are not fully our responsibility, and when they go wrong we can blame others for their advice, forgetting that, in fact, we chose to take it.

Clients who present for counseling have often had this experience. They may often feel they have lost their self-determination, lost in a world of confusion, where they don't know what the right thing is to do. These clients may present asking us to take the role of chief advisor, and this can be a strong pull, as they may be very strong in their expectation of this, and also it can at times seem to us to be fairly obvious what is going wrong. They may be giving their power away, have a very low sense of self-worth, be driven by a need for external approval, paralyzed by the fear of making the wrong decision. Our assumptions can be very wrong though, no matter how experienced we are, and so it is up to us, to resist the plea to do it for them, and to match the pace of the client, and allow them, in the safe space of their time with us, to explore the possibilities, unknown-ness and scary expanse of self-determination, and to claim it back as their birthright. We do best at this when we grapple with these ideas ourselves, for few of us are freely able to be truly self-determining, without looking to others and our community for direction.

The trap of victimhood

The idea of self determination brings me to the fraught and emotive area of victimhood. We, as psychologists, often see 'victims' — of crime, of accidents, of circumstance, of a mental illness, of a difficult childhood, of domestic violence. We see victims as having lost their self-determination through another's act. As a society we perpetrate this idea of victimhood. We believe victims can never fully recover, or, that if they can, then the crime wasn't so bad after all. The crime is judged depending on how badly the victim is affected. Can you see the problem here? If someone is resilient and survives a crime well, recovers quickly, we see that what happened to them may not have been so bad after all. This means that what has happened may not be fully acknowledged. The victim gets less support from society, and may even be criticized or seen as unnatural in their resilience. As a society we tend to make the victim dependent on our sympathy in the way our compensation systems and legal procedures function. This can have the effect of keeping them stuck, as they begin to rely on sympathy and start to identify with the events that occurred to them. They start to identify as being a victim, and being powerless.

We respond to events as we are taught to and as those in our society respond to them.

The way our society's justice system works relies on the idea of victimhood. In trying to get justice for a victim, the victim is forced to re-live their trauma, to focus on the negatives; what has been taken from them, how it has affected them and changed their lives for the worse. The more they become a victim, the more compensation they may receive.

How does this fit with our job? In looking for the best for our clients, we often look for the positives. How they have survived?

What strengths have enabled them to get through? We may use acceptance and work with clients to find how they can move on from any negative experience, and even grow and learn from it. Yet this is diametrically opposed to what they may be experiencing in wider society, and especially in the legal system if they are involved in that. Let's for a moment just drop this construct, and just imagine.

Imagine if we did not have this concept of irreparable damage. Events happen. People respond, there are actions and consequences. Events ARE as we perceive and interpret them.

Here is a simple example. In some parts of the world it is acceptable and normal for a girl to marry at puberty, say at 12, and have children soon after this. In our society this is considered neither acceptable nor normal. A 12-year-old girl who married and had children at 12 years old in western society would be considered a crime victim.

Two girls, one a crime victim, the other a normal member of her society, though we may still deplore her situation.

Are these girls equally victims? If not, why not? If so, are they equally affected by what has happened to them? Who is most likely to be more/least damaged by their experiences? Why? What are the factors that cause the damage? Ponder on this. What are your thoughts? Notice your judgment. What if there was no judgment, what would be there instead? Compassion? Love?

Of course the criminal act itself can cause huge damage, pain, shame and hurt, and I also believe that in addition to this, the response to, and interpretation of, this act by ourselves and our community is also of vital importance to how we see both the act and ourselves in relation to it. I have often pondered as I see fallout from negative events, on the damage that is done not simply from the event such as the commission of a crime, but also from our response and judgment as a society. I believe it is without doubt that much unnecessary damage is caused by the fear, shame and judgment in our response as a society.

An inspiring woman called Ingrid Poulson has written her story in a book called *Rise*. Her husband killed their two small children, and her father. In her book she has written the story of her journey through this. A voice rose up inside her and said, "I will not be brought so low." Perhaps from the same place came a knowing that she could choose to survive. She recognized her resilience and chose to rise to the challenge of going on, of rebuilding. She met with criticism at times—how could she survive this? A real mother would never recover, would die of grief, would never or could never move forward from this, but would be, should be even, stuck forever in a hellish world of grief and pain. This story really brought home to me how the victim can be punished by wider society when they do not respond in the appropriate victim fashion.

We believe in permanent damage, in things that are impossible to psychologically/spiritually recover from. Imagine just for a minute if we lost that belief? See the freedom suddenly created? The decrease in fear, the increase of hope, and trust. We are able to make these changes to society.

This is what brings me hope, what sends my heart soaring. The absolute belief that we are resilient, that we can overcome anything and that damage is never permanent. I know some of the ideas set out above are challenging, and perhaps it seems that I am absolving perpetrators of crime or cruelty of any responsibility, but this is not the case. I am aiming more to absolve those who are considered the victim. How long do they have to drag this around with them? When will we allow them to stop being a victim, and support them in finding a new identity?

The time is now, as we enter a new era, creating possibilities for a new way of being in the world. Imagine a world where there is equality, joy and harmony, a whole new idea of psychological health. Imagine the encouragement of all to be their best, to learn and strive and feel and love, and, yes, even fail, and be in mastery of self. This is something to really strive for and be part of. We are all living through the age of the most rapid change in history. It's time to harness the adaptability and openness to innovation of the times we are living in and apply changes to psychology to make it what we were drawn to in the beginning, a career of service to others, opening the way for them to strive to reach their potential, and in that way, also meeting our own.

Chapter 3

The therapist: introduction to working with energy

A man may imagine things that are false, but he can only understand things that are true, for if things be false, the apprehension of them is not understanding.
Isaac Newton

Therapy is only as effective as we, and the client, are prepared to make it. The client's part is best left to them, and we are well trained in assessing their level of commitment, discussing it in the session and working with this. Therapy, growth, and development are after all a matter of choice and, although generally seen as positive, they can be painful, scary, anxiety provoking and difficult. To manage this, a client must need to be committed, and feel that they are taking part out of their own free will.

We, however, are in a different situation. We must be committed to take part in the therapy of each of our clients, and we must be able to give our best in each moment. This does not mean working too hard, or giving away our energy—quite the contrary, in fact. It does, however, mean that we must be present, focused, attentive, flexible and aware. It also, especially, means that we must consistently work on our own growth and development as human beings. We must be willing, as our clients are, to take on the pain and fear and anxiety involved in growth, and embracing the new, in becoming more of who we are. Without this we are not giving our best, but are simply doing a job. We often see therapy as a one-way stream of benefit to our client, but there is so much to be gained for us, each day as we work with people, uncomfortable, worrying and difficult as it may sometimes be.

So, if we are stretching ourselves to this extent, and see all the hours in our lives, including our work hours, to be rich fodder for our own growth and learning, then we need to do as much and more than what we are expecting of our clients. I will expand over this chapter on some of the things that I am implementing in my own practice that make a great difference to me, and through me, to my clients.

Knowing yourself

This is a basic, one that has been encouraged from the beginning of the history of psychology and before. Some schools of therapy insist on regular therapy for the therapist, and certainly at the least all registered professionals who practice counseling are required to participate in regular supervision. We can take this so much further, and this is really a lifelong journey. Getting to know our triggers, blind spots, no-go zones is so important, and not only because these can become very obvious to our clients while we continue to ignore or deny them. This may not be professional, and could even be embarrassing, but my real concern here is that these things contribute to crippling our counseling ability, and our ability to make a difference, to see clearly, and to act as a mentor or a role model. We need to model for our clients. They need to see us practicing what we preach and walking the talk. Would you trust a therapist whose life was a mess or who clearly had no-go zones, or triggers, and was different whenever you saw them? Someone who could not exercise some control over their own emotions or their anxiety?

I'm not saying you can't be going through a divorce, or having family or work issues, after all, all our lives are messy, and we are certainly not immune. I'm simply talking about knowing yourself and being in control of yourself to the point where you are able to CHOOSE how to respond. Indeed, isn't this what we hope for most of our clients, that they understand that they can choose, that they have the power of a sense of agency. However, we must have it first to be able to show how it makes a difference. We need to know ourselves as intimately as possible, our emotions, fears, doubts and worries. In this way we continue to increase our own psychological clarity, and thereby constantly increase our ability to help make a difference for the people who seek our assistance. This is ongoing and lifelong work.

Energetic awareness

Whether we know it or not we are always dealing with energy in our practice. How many times have you come out of a session feeling drained, or been exhausted when you got home, even irritable or snappy and there's no good reason for it. When you look back to see what could be wrong, you determine that you had a good day, clients made progress, no big dramas. So what's the matter?

Have you found yourself dreading certain clients, and hoping they don't make their appointment, but you can't explain why? And then on top of this the guilty feeling that you shouldn't be feeling like this, and that they are perfectly nice people who are coming to you for help, and paying you. Wow! No wonder you're tired, and no doubt flirting with the idea of cutting down your practice to less days a week or less hours a day. Looking at the idea of energy and energy exchange will help make some of these feelings more understandable.

The way I see energy is this: it is a constant interplay between ourselves, and all those we interact with. It is a way to assess how people are in the moment, what they may need, and a way of communicating. Psychologists and therapists who work with people daily are good at this but do not necessarily see what they do as energy work. They may call it 'reading' people, or noticing the atmosphere, or the mood of the person. When we become very attuned to energy it can both help and hinder us in practice.

What is 'energy' in the therapeutic context? Let's look at some common important concepts in counseling and see how the idea of energy fits in.

The Therapeutic relationship

There are three important entities in the room during an individual counseling session. These are the therapist, the client, and the relationship between the two, the therapeutic relationship.

We all know by now that research has shown that the one necessary thing in successful therapy is a good therapeutic relationship. No one particular counseling model has been found to be better than others in general, though some are considered more effective with particular types of clients, but the one thing we cannot be without is a good rapport and a strong relationship with the client.

So, what exactly does this consist of, and how do we create it?

Good relationships are often based on liking. This can be a treacherous path, as often people like us when they can get what they want from us. It isn't unusual that you find counselors in a cycle of giving away all their energy to clients in a kind of 'fix-it' mode, or simply feeling sympathy, and getting caught up in the client's story, being on their side, against others. In this way we often donate our energy to clients and end up drained and exhausted, doing a lot of hard work and even fighting battles that aren't ours. Building rapport and relationship simply on liking is untenable in the long term, because it means we are relying on the client to approve of us, and like what we do. When we lose their approval, perhaps in a situation where we may be challenging them, or refusing to enter their story, this means that the relationship may then disintegrate. We need to build a relationship that is stronger than this, more unconditional.

Starting with using some of what can be called psycho-spiritual qualities will help develop trust. Acceptance, compassion and unconditional positive regard will establish a platform where the client feels safe, and where the relationship can remain strong, even through challenging the client, their discomfort and their anger.

As therapists we need to constantly hold an awareness of the therapeutic relationship. We often discuss it in the therapy room, and also in supervision, but even when it is not on the table overtly, we need to know what is happening in this space, as this directs much of our work. I see this relationship as a constant interaction of feeling, mood, communication, especially nonverbal communication, and energy. When we are in relationship with people, we start to be able to know how they are feeling, understand how to respond in the most appropriate way, and we can feel the quality of our interaction, how strong or weak the connection is; any hostility or positive feeling. The space between us is full of energy flow and crackles with feeling, communication, and interaction. For me this is, without a doubt, a way of working with energy. Our relationship is energy, and our reactions and responses to others are often the product of energy. We adjust what we are doing and how we are working according to how this space is, and what fills it. This is a matter of 'feeling into' the space, and working with that feeling. I think this is a particularly accurate way to frame it as the word 'empathy' is derived from the Greek ἐμπάθεια (empatheia), meaning 'to feel into'. If we are constantly placing some of our attention on the relationship with the client, onto the 'feeling into' how we are working together, a lot of what we feel may be used as information to let us know how therapy is progressing, and how safe, and how supported the client feels.

As we practice and become more confident we tend to work more this way, which I think is also why many, or even most therapists do not tend to use one single therapy approach with all their clients, or even within the treatment of a single client.

We use the word eclectic, but I suspect that, as we become more experienced, we take everything we learn and create our own unique approach. It may be that there are as many treatment approaches as there are therapists. Irvin Yalom, in his book *The Gift of Therapy*, talks about creating a new therapy for each client. Part of the magic of this approach is the ability to work with the changing energies of the relationship and the space between.

Creating a space

Therapists often talk about "creating a space." So what does it mean? To me it means creating a time and a place where people are safe (and importantly *feel* safe) to talk about and address whatever they feel the need to. It means maintaining this safety for the client, which is about an attitude of non-judgment and compassion. It means that we have worked on our own psychological clarity and triggers, so that they do not intrude on this time and place. If something comes up it stays firmly outside the door until the session is over. Creating a space also means the practitioner stepping out of it. Giving the client space for what they need. This can be difficult, as we often have session plans, or places we want to get to with a client, but the more of an agenda we have, the more space we take up, so we have to let go of these expectations, and stay open to what happens in the moment. Feeling the urge to help or fix is also an agenda. If we feel we need to please the client, or feel ourselves to be useful, to get some kind of outcome, then our own needs intrude into the session. In this case the space we take up is even larger, filled as it is with our own anxiety and urgency. When this happens be aware, release the need and expectation and step back out of the space so the client can fill it. Once the space is created and you have stepped out of it, it is still important to maintain a presence. The client needs to feel held in a safe, compassionate and loving space, not just any old space! A strong and supportive counseling presence simply requires attention, focus, compassion and acceptance. It is useful to start becoming aware of, and then practicing, radiating these qualities into the space. Other qualities may also be helpful. Ones I often use are trust (in self as well as in the client), hope, serenity and patience, depending on what is appropriate, there are many others. This can take a bit of practice to get right, as it's NOT about forcing this on the client. It is simply holding a presence and a space which the client is free to take or leave. It does not need to be verbalized, or forced. It is about simply being.

When I first started private practice I felt quite anxious about what I was offering clients. Sessions felt difficult, not what I was used to when I worked in education and hospital settings. I worried about whether the client was getting their money's worth. I soon realized that all this anxiety, and trying to be the best therapist ever was getting in the way of the counseling. I tried too hard and did too much, and this meant there was hardly any room for the client to move. I realized I was making the session all about me. The more I did this and the harder I tried the less effective the sessions were, and on top of that they were exhausting. So much hard work! I had lost the feeling of allowance, and acceptance. I was trying to push the client faster so they would be happy with their progress. As I realized this and managed my anxiety better, I remembered to step out of the way again. Once my anxiety was left outside the door, I was able to make the session about them, to hold a space for them, to allow them to set the pace, and even, if they chose, to get nothing out of it. With that change there was such a difference, an ease and grace and flow to the sessions, and the creation of an opportunity for the client to really unfold.

So, as we acknowledge or become aware that in our daily work with clients, and indeed in all of our daily life, we are constantly coming into contact with other people's energy, and that this energy effects us, some questions then arise.

What can we do about it?

How can we work with it?

How can we control the impact on ourselves and others?

It might be helpful to see this in terms of maintaining boundaries. We are all familiar with the importance of professional boundaries. We keep sessions to time, are not available on call 24 hours a day, do not socialize with clients, and do not divulge inappropriate personal information. We maintain physical and emotional boundaries with our clients. We may set limits on physical contact as we see fit, and certainly on emotional entanglement.

Energetic boundaries are equally essential. We must manage where our energy goes and what we get affected by. Energy flows are two-way. You may often feel exhausted at the end of a day with clients, or even after just one client. This would indicate that you are giving a lot of yourself and your energy to those clients. This energy may be expended in worry for the client, or sympathy, it may be in fighting off their expectation, or in feeling the need to excuse or explain yourself. There may also be some feelings like guilt, perhaps you feel that you should be doing more. The other thing to be aware of is taking on energy such as anxiety, urgency, worry or moods from your clients. It is important to have enough time between clients to check in with yourself, and how you are feeling; to notice if there is anything left from your last client that you should let go of, so that you do not pass that into your next session. So, how to do it?

Chapter 4

Working with energy part 2: maintaining energetic boundaries

I can't change the direction of the wind but I can adjust my sails to reach my destination.
Jimmy Dean

How to maintain energetic boundaries

From reading the previous chapter you can see that we work with energy all the time in counseling. This then makes it imperative that we become energy literate. We must start to become aware not only of the way our clients, and indeed, everyone around us, are using their energy, but also how we are using our own.

Exploring these ideas, and increasing my own awareness around the use of energy, and the use of the simple energetic hygiene process given at the end of this chapter, has enhanced not only my practice, but also my well-being to a greater extent than I could have imagined.

I don't know any psychologist, or indeed any helping professional who has not at some point struggled to understand how not to be completely drained of all energy at the end of a day seeing clients. Some clients are more draining than others, and it is not uncommon for therapists to dread seeing certain clients.

My concerns are that sometimes in our quest to find ways to deal with this, we can cut off from clients to the point that the therapeutic relationship suffers, because we almost completely withdraw our presence from the session, either as a way to hold boundaries, or simply by wishing the hour away, thus not being in the here and now.

I remember when I was working in a methadone clinic; I had

a particular client that I would dread so much that I would hide when he came in for his dose in case he caught sight of me and wanted to see me. I would come home drained and irritable, and I started to think I couldn't do my job. In a way I was right. I wasn't very effective, but it wasn't about my skills or ability, it was because I had no idea how to protect myself, and conserve my energy for myself. Once I started doing a basic 'energetic hygiene' daily, as well as being stronger with my boundaries, things changed dramatically. I could see clients without giving up all my own energy, I got less caught up in their stories and feeling sorry for them, so therefore I felt less urgency and anxiety, and so I was in fact a far more effective counselor for them. The energetic boundaries also allowed me to maintain my other boundaries more effectively, such as sticking to appointment times, and being far less able to be manipulated as I was far less open to their expectations and agendas. The guilty feeling of not doing enough, and never being able to, was gone. I discovered that was my clients' (and of course not all of them) projection. Now I am out of the drug and alcohol field, working in private practice and with adolescents, but still these practices are all-important. The force of a client's expectations can be strong, and the disapproval and disappointment when they are not met can really bring down confidence as well as make us feel a sense of urgency to fix the issue. When we keep our boundaries high we are far more able to see unrealistic expectations for what they are. We can allow the client to feel as they feel, and for them to choose to work with us, or to let them seek another therapist that is more to their liking.

How to hold boundaries and yet not cut off

There can be a concern that as we endeavor to maintain appropriate boundaries with clients we can actually end up cutting off from them, creating a wall between us that blocks out all energetic interaction, and of course leads to a deterioration of the relationship, or an inability to build a strong therapeutic relationship in the first place. A way to avoid this is to put into practice a couple of ideas.

Consider the way you usually operate and respond to people, in both your personal and professional life. Usually people find that they respond to people, not according to how those people are in the moment, but according to how they feel themselves, in the moment. What that means is that if you are feeling 'good' that day—open or happy, you will be more open, indiscriminately, to other people.

An example of this is coming home after a really enjoyable day. You are happy and content and feeling good. You arrive home and greet your family member or housemate. You soon discover that they, unlike you, are in a bad mood after a difficult day. You notice this, but still remain open and vulnerable, try to talk them into a better mood and within a few minutes you are arguing, or perhaps you simply start feeling different, less joyful, your good mood slowly melting away, to reflect your partner's.

Wouldn't it make more sense to respond to people according to how *they* are in the moment? This would mean having boundaries that are appropriate in each moment according to the people you are dealing with. So, in the above case you would come home, notice your partner's mood, and set your boundaries to allow them to be as they are, but not to affect you. How they feel is not your reality. This is what I mean when I talk of boundaries of "unconditional love and above." These boundaries mean that all you let in and all you let out is unconditional love. If you are not feeling great you maintain responsibility for not spreading that around, and if others are not feeling great, you raise your boundaries to not let that in.

Think of a medieval walled city, able to protect itself if necessary in times of danger. If the ruler of that city set the defenses of the city according to how he felt at the time, the danger of being invaded would be enormous. The ruler could believe himself enlightened, believe in peace among all people and tear down the walls in preparation for utopia. In the likely scenario that the waiting army outside may not share his vision, you can imagine the consequences! Instead the ruler must set the defenses of the city according to how the outsiders are in the moment, whether they are peaceful and wish to trade, or whether they are aggressive and wish to invade.

Thinking of energetic interactions in terms of cords

I have found the concept of cords between people really useful in my work, both for myself, and for my clients. The concept is this. Imagine that there is an energetic cord between you and everyone you have a relationship with. These cords are created as soon as your attention is focused on someone, such as in conversation, and remain, until you, or they, consciously decide to 'cut' them. This concept helps explain in a visual and concrete way, how other people's moods can affect your own, and even how we are able to connect into how others are feeling. As therapists, these cords are both a tool and a burden. They help us connect to the client, and work with them, to get a sense of how they are feeling, but if we are not vigilant about our awareness of the cords, and of cutting them, we can continue to be affected by the client. This is also true in our personal lives, with our friends and families. I have found the the visualization of cutting these imaginary cords to be a powerful tool in my own practice, and indeed my personal life, as well as being useful for clients. I have found that it can be an immediate way to remove any anxiety, urgency, guilt or worry that I may have taken on from another person.

When working with clients, and especially adolescents, the idea of boundaries, cords between people, and the concept of taking on other people's feelings really rings a bell for them. The imagery helps them visualize creating energetic boundaries and allows them to differentiate themselves, and how they feel, from others and feelings that do not actually belong to them. Adults also benefit from these ideas, and I find that using the 'energetic hygiene' process given below really helps me through my day, and prevents me losing my own energy so I can end the day feeling energized and light, rather than dragged down, exhausted and burnt out. Skuvholt in his book *The Resilient Practitioner* puts it this way, "one essence of attachment for counselors... is to be a highly skilled relationship maker who constantly attaches, is involved and separates well" (p13). This is a wonderful description of what happens with energetic connections and successful cord cutting, expressed rather differently.

It is not just with clients that we create cords. We have strong cords connecting us to all people in our lives. It is equally important to keep these cords clear as well, so that we do not get tangled up and confused in other people's emotions, needs and issues. Keeping cords clear helps keep you clear and helps you to be able to be sure that what you are feeling or going through is actually yours, not something from someone else. Clarity is important for all, but especially so for those who work closely with people as we do, and noticing how these 'cords' operate in your life can be very helpful in creating and fostering awareness, in practice and in life.

Clues that you have cords and connections which are affecting you

'Compassion fatigue', burnout and exhaustion are considered some of the professional hazards of the helping professions. You can see how these states would be created or exacerbated by an unawareness and neglect of energetic connections and cords. Often poor relationships with clients are born out of the shutdown that can accompany feeling overwhelmed by the cords and connections you may be carrying or creating with your clients.

It is likely that throughout your work with a client you will have these cords that connect you to them. This is why it is important to visualize cutting these regularly, as they are reinstated when you see them or communicate with them. These cords, or connections, are, as I have mentioned, not necessarily negative in the sense that they can help us do our job better. Through this exchange of energy we get a good idea of how the client is feeling and we are able to feel the state of the relationship and rapport between ourselves and the client. However, if the cords are not kept clear between sessions we may start noticing more negative repercussions from these connections. These might present in the form of intrusive thoughts about particular clients, including worrying excessively, anxiety, urgency in sessions, dreaming of clients, and feelings that seem like they don't 'fit' with you. Poor client outcomes, ill health, exhaustion, depression, as well as poor or unprofessional relationships with clients are other possibilities.

Of course these feelings are not always to do with our connections to the clients. Many of these feelings can happen due to our own issues. This is why it is important to keep as clear as possible.

A good experiment to do if you are dubious about whether these connections can really have these effects is to do the cord clearing I describe below, and see if and how it changes things. You may be surprised!

Energetic boundaries exercise

Find a quiet space where you can spend five minutes doing this process each morning, perhaps the shower, your bedroom or your office before your first client, or even between each client. If at any time you start to feel harried, rushed or anxious throughout the day, you may want to do all or part of it again.

This is also an excellent exercise to give clients to use

within their own lives.

Imagine strong cords, like roots, coming out of your feet and rooting you firmly into the center of the earth, so you feel grounded and stable.

Set boundaries so that you are open only to vibrations of unconditional love or above, so that anything below this within you, stays within you, and anything below this outside of you will not be taken on by you. Keep checking in with these boundaries regularly.

Imagine a golden protective bubble around you which protects you from all that is not in, of and for love.

Imagine being surrounded by a violet flame, which burns up all fear and transforms it into love.

Imagine nets made of gold and platinum threads running through your energy system clearing all fear and debris, old thoughts and rubbish from the past away.

Imagine a cylinder of light coming down around you like a cookie cutter, cutting all cords and connections to others that are not of and for love.

Imagine a wide column of light that comes from as high as you can reach into the core of the universe, and passes through and over you like a wide spotlight from above and goes right into the core of the earth. Within this column of light feel yourself align to the values of love and truth.

Feel yourself center in your heart.

Allow yourself to be present, here, now.

Allow the creative source within to choose its own knowing.

Affirm that you welcome and honor your feelings (no matter what they are).

Acknowledge that you create your own reality.

Flood your heart with the feeling of gratitude and allow yourself to release any judgment you may be holding on to.

Affirm that you choose love, wisdom and compassion.

Release all energy that is not of you, and not of love, back to its original source with love.

Allow yourself to harmonize with these new choices.

Chapter 5

Being of service and creating meaning

Who looks outside dreams, who looks inside awakens.
Carl Jung

The most effective way to help is to allow people to do their own learning in their own time.

The hardest thing is stopping most of what we are doing. We need to do less. And the first thing we need to do (or not do) is to not judge or expect for our client. This sounds obvious. Most of us do not judge our clients, it's true, but many of us judge what has happened to them or where they are at (a difficult place) or how they are feeling (they need to feel better). This does not feel like judgment because we feel aligned with the client, but it is, and it leads to a sense of urgency and anxiety for us as we then get shunted along the track of trying to make things better and to try to move the client to a better place. So, if *we* are judging them, it will not be possible for *them* to stop the judgment of themselves, as they take their cue from us.

The absolute basic fundamental thing we initially do for our client is hold a space of non-judgment and unconditional positive regard. We need to be fully accepting of where they are, how long they stay there and what they are feeling, thereby allowing them to release any judgment or expectation they may have placed upon themselves about their progress, what's 'wrong' with them, how long it's taking, and how they are different to everybody else. This is all about creating a safe and roomy space for the client to move, explore and learn. This sounds easy, but as therapists we know how hard it can be to hold onto yourself in a session, to do less rather than more, to take up less space and to be rather than do. This is the magic, the value and the rarity of therapy. What happens in a good therapy session almost never happens in daily life, and the space created for contemplation and exploration can achieve miracles.

It takes training, experience, trust and hope to be able to facilitate this kind of space for the client, and not to jump in and fix or to 'help' in the way this word is usually meant. The difficulty is that the very people who are drawn to the field of counseling, psychology, social work or other helping professions are often, by nature, helpers. This is what we want to do, and it is our biggest downfall as well as our greatest strength. Often our anxiety can rise when we feel we need to help or fix, because this need to help, to 'do something' can lead us to a sense of hopelessness where we end up feeling powerless to help, we simply don't know what to do. If we are looking for something to do then indeed we are often powerless when it comes to 'fixing' the problem, or doing it for them. Sometimes even though we understand with our mind that holding a space and creating room for the client to move through their own problems at their own pace is the best way we can help, it often feels like we are doing nothing, and perhaps not giving value to our client. We doubt our understanding of what helping really is in a counseling context, and may often, at the same time, feel a real pull from our clients for us to fix them or help them. It is these moments that can catapult us into taking over the session, giving advice, talking a lot, or adopting an agenda. This is tiring and can be dispiriting. I have often heard counselors wonder whether they are doing a good job, or whether they should retrain, perhaps as an accountant or, often, a florist! I too have often, in previous moments, found myself wishing I were a waitress, or anything but a therapist in these high anxiety moments.

It is not because we are bad at what we do, that these doubts and fantasies creep in, but because, sometimes briefly, sometimes more permanently, we lose trust in ourselves, and in the value of therapy as it is meant to be. We give into our anxiety and predisposition to 'help' and wade in boots and all. Although we are doing this with the best of intentions, it shows a lack of respect to the client, an inability to accept them at the pace they are going, and even a lack of confidence that they are equipped to find their own solutions.

Our need and desire to help can be funneled into the more helpful and more profound idea of being of service. When we place trust in our client and their process then our role becomes clearer. It is to facilitate the best and most effective learning and growth for the client, and this may not be what we think it is. The question to hold in our hearts is simply, "How may I be of service?" while working towards the clients highest good and potential. Of great importance are the practices of understanding, holding compassion and acceptance.

One of the most distinguished characteristics of our profession is our intense focusing on highly skilled perspective taking: a combination of empathy, perceptual flexibility, tolerance for ambiguity and affective sensitivity. When successful, all of this translates into a profound ability to understand the world as other people understand it. This well honed ability, one of our occupational strengths, is not possessed by many people in other occupations. (Skovholt, 2000, p.2)

Awareness and presence in the here and now is what makes this possible. As soon as we worry about doing something or focus on where we want to be instead of where we are, with a sense of urgency we are no longer in the here and now, but have projected forward to some other place, and this makes it almost impossible to move forward from our true location. I often think of it like this: Imagine you were hiking, using a map. You are trying to find part of a valley that has a great camping spot by a beautiful stream. If you are not clear about where in the valley you currently are (even if it isn't where you want to be), then getting to that stream will be nearly impossible. It is only when we know and accept where we are that we can start to move towards a new place of our choice. This is true for both client and therapist. Transferring this idea to everyday life, it is easy to see that people regularly can be in denial about how they feel or what's going on for them because they don't want it to be that way. This makes progress for them so much harder as they strike out blindly from that place to try and find a better place, but are unable to use any kind of map usefully as they do not have a true starting off point. So it makes sense that before any useful therapy can start there first must be exploration and discovery of the truth of where that person is, allowing awareness, and always staying in the here and now. The space of acceptance we create as therapists allows these clients to bravely explore these areas and develop their own acceptance for themselves which then gives them the tools to move forward to a different place, of their choice, and in their own empowerment. It is important that the therapist maintains this awareness also, and does not fall into urgency for the client to improve or get better.

It is important to monitor when we feel any urgency in terms of helping the client move on, or worrying about them being in a bad way. Obviously it is part of our responsibility to do what we can to prevent harm, and there are times when an active intervention, such as a more directive approach, or even calling in authorities may be necessary, but it is important to remember that a deep level of acceptance from us, as their therapist, that wherever they are is okay, is magic in allowing the client to accept that themselves. In that acceptance they will be less distressed and better able to self-soothe and manage their emotions.

If we are able to successfully hold our clients in a space of acceptance, understanding and compassion without agenda then we will be able to really make use of a simple precept a teacher of mine once told me, "Take no credit; take no blame."

When I first heard this it felt like this could be a total abdication of responsibility. Over time though, as I explored the idea, I realized that if at any point we as therapists feel we should take credit or blame for a client's progress, then we have an agenda and a bias, and will be unable to be fully in acceptance with that client. It means we will be taking up space in the room with our need for the treatment to work well, according to us, to have a 'success.' This of course sounds like a laudable aim. Yes, we all want to be able to have clients make progress, but this is not about us, it is about the client. That is and should be our interest. Our responsibility as professional therapists is to give the client the safe space to do what would be of greatest service to them, providing tools when necessary, creating awareness and being in complete acceptance, understanding and compassion. It is about being, not doing.

Be as clear as you can be

Keeping the energy of the space between clear is as important as creating it in the first place. It makes a real difference to both practitioner and client. It is important to be conscious of what we are doing with our own energy, so that the client has room to explore, without taking on any of what we may have got going on because the energy exchange can go two ways. We may have our own issues going on in our personal lives that we need to leave outside the door, so that the space we provide is not infected by that. It is also important, as mentioned earlier, to keep it clear of a sense of urgency or anxiety that we may be feeling. This does not mean we will not at times feel these things, but we keep it firmly with us rather than leaking out into the session, or preferably clear it using the magic of acceptance, and feeling without judgment of ourselves as well as our clients.

As well as keeping the space clear from the more 'negative' stuff, it is also important that we keep it clear from what we

43

see as the more positive stuff. If we keep donating energy to the client they do not get any long-term gain, and we will probably end up exhausted and resentful. In order to be real, the progress of the client must rely fully on him or herself and not on any energy we may have donated in order to fix, help or palliate.

Donating energy is very different to holding a space of non-judgment, acceptance and unconditional positive regard. I talked earlier about the usefulness of radiating energy in the form of qualities such as hope and compassion, but donating energy is a very different thing. Radiating is as the sun radiates heat. It is unaffected whether we bask in its warmth or not, and us doing so does not deplete the sun. Donating on the other hand is giving away from our own energy reserves and it does both affect and deplete us. Donating our energy usually comes from our own need to help and fix which is an agenda albeit a seemingly altruistic one. Needing someone to get better, to the point that we are giving them our own energy to do that is an indication that there is a judgment we have placed on where the client is right now. This is a great opportunity to release the judgment and practice acceptance.

It takes a brave therapist to step back, allow things to be as they are and yet still bear witness and provide a safe space for a client to struggle and hurt and grow. We are geared to fix and for most of us, fixing and helping means doing, and the more the better.

But there is nothing more empowering for the client than truly believing in themselves—that they can handle it, that they are able to manage, and that you still provide a judgment free space of support and attention for them to do this. This builds their confidence and self-esteem in a way that being fixed never could.

We may need to get rid of our clever tricks and magical symptom relief. Some practitioners rely on a mask of greatness—

greater knowledge, greater understanding, a perceived ability to mind read, and to know the right thing to do. This mask can lead to magical cures, those that seem too good to be true, too quick, too easy. This mask is not always put on by the therapist; it can be projected by the client, and either way, it can be important to spend the time to remove it, discuss it, explore it as seems most appropriate as these magical cures provide no empowerment or agency to the client, and no lasting fix.

Our big words and sometimes magic-seeming 'techniques' may need to be left behind for us to become more real in what we do. This may mean we don't get the credit and that psychology loses the mask of mystery and magic that it seems to hold. A case in point for the aura of mystery and magic is the number of times I have been asked whether I can read minds when I say I am a psychologist.

It is courageous, to remove the mystery, and the extra stuff that as a profession we have added over a hundred or so years, perhaps because we felt inadequate, or unable to explain why what we do helps, so we decided to make it more complicated. Therapy is a complex pursuit that may, to some, seem easy and there may be much criticism from those who don't understand this, as there has been in the past and the present.

It is time for us to have pride and confidence in what we provide as a service for people in their quest to grow and learn and be the best they can be. As professionals we have come of age, and do not have to hide the skill of what we do behind a shroud of mystery because we fear it is not enough. It is enough. It is the privilege to help facilitate change and to support human development.

Of course there is more to do than simply sitting and being supportive, clearing the space and removing judgment and expectation. But what a start! We can still use all those hard earned therapy and counseling techniques doing most of what we do already but transform it by clearing ourselves of judgment and expectation, familiarizing ourselves with energy, interaction and exchange, and encouraging our clients to do the same. Our clients may need or ask for guidance or a mentoring approach, one which is more directive but still allowing the client to do the work, judgment and expectation free.

Aligning and Centering

As mindfulness has become mainstream and books like Eckhart Tolle's *The Power Of Now* become bestsellers, more and more we hear phrases such as 'being here now', 'grounding oneself' or even 'align and center.' I'd like to discuss the usefulness of some of these ideas, because I have found that using them, simple as they are, can affect psychological practice profoundly. Aligning and centering are two basic practices that once you use them, you would never be without.

As a therapist, when you are in alignment, you are 'in the zone', in flow, and in the present moment. This alone makes for great therapy as you are able to move with where the client is going and be fully present and attentive to them. I need to clarify here, that when I talk about alignment, I am not using it in the traditional counseling sense of being in alignment with a client, i.e., on their side, I am talking about being in alignment with yourself, your intentions and your goals.

To feel aligned, take a few moments to ground yourself and be in the present moment. Feel yourself as balanced and in place. Take a few moments to sense this feeling; notice where you might feel out of alignment—not just physically, but emotionally, mentally and spiritually. Allow all these aspects to be in tune and working on the same team. Practice this regularly, whenever you can, but especially before and between clients.

Once you have this as part of your practice you will be able to work with your client far more effectively, being always present and in the moment, and you will also be able to teach them this skill as part of the therapy will be for the client to witness this, and learn both actively and passively how to bring this into their own lives for their own benefit. Ideally you would start with teaching the client to be in alignment as much as possible, even just for the therapy hour, and then continue from there. The more alignment, the more effective the work. It can help at first to imagine standing in the middle of a wide pillar of light that is anchored at both ends—deep within the earth, like a root, and up into the depths of space. With this kind of wide, strong alignment, you feel physically steadier, posture is better. Emotions are easier to regulate and the busy mind is easier to control. It is a function of being more present.

Alignment is linked closely to centering, and the one helps with the other. Centering helps bring us back to our hearts. As qualified therapists we have usually completed years of academic training, and we are in the habit of coming from our heads, so it is good to get into practice with being back in the heart, as it is always where the best sessions and the most profound turning points in therapy come from.

To feel centered, put your attention and perception into your heart area; feel what it's like to come from there. Keep practicing this. Remind yourself to bring yourself back there. Teach yourself to come from this heart center, for it is the true center of your being, and the place from which you can truly steer and respond with wisdom and compassion and love.

Teaching yourself to be centered in the heart allows a greater presence and stillness, which is hugely beneficial in therapy, for the client and for yourself. It helps you to maintain a steady level of energy and not get exhausted, or be unable to give the last client of the day your best. It also helps you be aware of the energetic interplay between you and the client, it helps to hold boundaries and creates greater awareness. There is a sense of peace and stillness inside which is radiated to others; this helps facilitate the sense of safety and relationship so necessary to the successful practice of psychology and counseling. Practice this

47

by reminding yourself to keep bringing yourself back to your heart. It is your true home. Teaching this to clients helps them to still their mind, respond rather than react and allows there to be greater awareness of themselves and their environment.

Chapter 6

Failure and letting go of the past

Success is not final, failure is not fatal: it is the courage to continue that counts.
Winston Churchill

Failure is misnamed. In many ways, failure is success. We MUST fail in order to grow and learn. We often see failure as something that can be avoided and should be at all costs, but all this does is keep us safe and small, and far from embodying all that we could do and be. Only those who can fail well, even spectacularly, are able to really succeed. There have been studies done and papers written on the importance of failure in learning, but I would like to extrapolate this idea to something even more integral, more human.

We feel we have failed when we are feeling the wrong way (angry instead of calm, or sad instead of happy), or are not well liked, or are disapproved of. We feel we failed when things have not gone according to plan, and everything seems like it is in a huge mess. This feeling of failure is all about judgment. We judge ourselves and our feelings and even our human-ness. We judge unpleasant emotions and we judge unpleasant events. Somehow they are the fault of either ourselves or others and they should not exist. This leads us to fight them, deny them, suppress them or ignore them. Sound familiar? Notice this in practice with clients? What a relief when some acceptance is simply introduced. There is so much more space to move when the judgment is removed. We need to acknowledge the feelings and events, before we can explore them they have to exist for us first. Once they do and we suspend judgment, even as an exercise, we can then move to get to know ourselves, unpeel some of our values and ideas and start to see patterns in how we respond and react in our lives. Mainstream psychology and counseling is already familiar with some of these ideas. We see them expounded by practitioners of Mindfulness, ACT, Positive Psychology and DBT. These newer ideas have changed the face of psychology in the last couple of decades, and have opened us, as psychologists, up to new ideas and ways of being; opened us up to ideas such as acceptance, compassion and gratitude and the power of these in the healing of others.

Mindfulness teaches us to notice and observe our feelings and to suspend judgment of them. It allows us to be aware of that part of ourselves that is not caught up in the maelstrom of self-doubt and worry which then anchors us and creates a stable base by which we can process whatever is going on for us.

ACT (acceptance and commitment therapy) debunks the idea that we must get rid of all our negative feelings before we can be happy, or be effective, or be 'fixed.' It teaches that all kinds of feelings can be happening for us, and it is not about changing them because they are bad, it is about accepting them, learning not to fight them, freeing ourselves up to have those feelings and still function as we wish to. The acceptance here, letting go of the judgment, is the key to allowing us to move on. As we often see in practice, clients often feel stuck, and this is usually because they cannot let go of a judgment. The simple act of letting go allows movement again.

Positive Psychology reminded us to put some focus back on the positive, to spend some time giving that attention rather than the traditional focus of what was going wrong, what the 'failure' was. Of course this is often necessary, but it doesn't need to be at the expense of affirming also what may be going well. Some tools Positive Psychology uses to address this are focusing on strengths, and re-orienting people towards gratitude, through discussion in session and also through gratitude logs. We will discuss gratitude in more depth later.

DBT, Dialectical Behavior Therapy introduces the idea of

radical acceptance *coupled with* the need to change, and this supports the idea that before we can make changes we must accept, and release the judgment on, the way things are. After that we can move freely. Avoidance and denial leaves us where we are.

These approaches, and those like them, have been a massive turnaround for western psychology, and I think we can go even further.

These approaches encourage us to align and center ourselves. To breathe, focus, become aware of our bodies in space, and this enables us to be in a space of allowance—to notice how we feel, how our mind is chattering, and what is going on underneath. This allowing enables the feelings we have to come more strongly to the surface, to be felt, and if desired, let go.

At this point usually our clients, and ourselves when we also use these processes, are feeling whatever may be coming to the surface. This, with further application of mindfulness then passes, and something else comes to take its place. But what about if WE ourselves are able to choose what takes its place? There is so much power in this, and so much wonder in the experience of choosing, when we first see that we have control over this choice.

One of the things we encourage in clients is a sense of agency. How better to instill this and make this concrete than for them to choose their own feelings. To ask, and answer the questions: What will most benefit me and my higher purpose, and move me towards where I want to be? This is not about suppressing emotions, it is about letting go of the past and moving towards, rather than away from. As this process is applied, and judgment is released, the past is also released and room is created for a new feeling, one which we can choose and decide on for ourselves, as a resource for our growth and learning, and getting to where we want to go. Try it, and see how powerful it is. It can only be done once the other feeling has been processed and released.

We see clients on a daily basis who have developed often very sophisticated strategies to facilitate their own survival, or avoid what they are most afraid of. These patterns and strategies have been most helpful, as they have aided survival, and got them to where they are now. There comes a time though, as we know, where these have become not only obsolete but a hindrance. Often by this time they have forgotten that they are the creators of the strategy, and so feel helpless to let go, they forget they have the power to release it when it no longer serves them. We need to work on clearing our own similar patterns, to be able to have a discussion with the client on where they think their own hindrances are, what their purpose is/was, and how to overcome it now. We, and they, need to become detectives seeking out and releasing these patterns that are no longer helpful.

Releasing the judgment and re-choosing exercise

As you release the judgment, you will notice that the feeling changes or even disappears. It is time to consciously re-choose what to put in its place. Practice choosing a state of being; choose how it would feel to embody this state of being. This can be anything you feel would serve your highest potential. Things like compassion, kindness, acceptance, self-acceptance, worthiness, unconditional love, joy, courage and optimism are all great choices. There are many more. Feel for yourself what would be most appropriate in the moment. If you allow it to, the feeling will present itself to be chosen. Call in that feeling and allow it to flood your heart. Give it time if you need to, to settle. Use the list of qualities to help you choose.

Letting go of the past

How difficult it can be to let go of the past and how destructive when we don't. As psychologists and therapists, when we work with clients we are privileged to receive lessons in this daily. We can see, so easily in others, how keeping hold of the past hinders them from living now. We see the fears that come into play that stop them moving forward. We see people who are living the same pattern over and over, for example: abuse, violence, self-destructive relationships, relationship-destroying patterns in families and many other things which may be much less dramatic such as running away from commitment, patterns of emotional reactions, not staying in any job long, or having affairs. When we see this, what we are witnessing is the past recurring over and over. The person is consulting their memory of the past, their own personal history book for what they did in this situation last time and doing it again. Choosing something new is challenging and frightening, and often there can be a sense that our response is the correct one and will have the desired outcome one day.

I believe we all do this to some level, but it is usually only the individuals who are really stuck, often in many areas, that come and seek our help. I treat these visits as true gifts to me, as it reminds me of where I too am getting stuck and living in the past, and allows me opportunity to reflect in my own time on how I can let go.

The transformation involved when you see someone truly let go of the past is incredible. The progress they make in therapy can leave you gasping. I had a client who was so ready to let go of the past that she started in our first session and made the most amazing strides by our second that I thought she must be simply trying to please me. I couldn't believe all that she was saying, but it continued through session after session. In a couple of weeks her attitude to work changed, her relationship with her husband transformed, and his behavior completely altered, her worries and anxieties that she felt were paralyzing her left. I certainly can't take any of the credit. It was all about her letting go of the past. As I mentioned earlier it is never for us to take the credit, or indeed the blame. The simplicity of what we do is to create space to facilitate the exploration of another human being into their own complexities. We can help facilitate and encourage change in others, but never create it.

The courage of the clients I see is an inspiration for me to make the changes in my own life, to let go of the past and to be worthy of those who come to me for therapy. Clients are my constant stretch, they create the impetus to be the best I can be, and every time they take me out of my comfort zone I learn so much more and I am grateful.

Why do we all, to some degree or another, hang on to the past? It's often unpleasant, many things went wrong, and yet we seem to want to drag it with us until the end of our days.

I believe it's at least partly about fear of the new. The old saying, "better the devil you know." We know we have survived the past, difficult as it might have been. The risk in taking a new path into the unknown feels too great. Our very survival feels at stake. The impetus to let go of the past can come in a number of ways. First, when someone is so SICK of the old that they don't care if they don't survive the new, they just can't possibly go through all that stuff AGAIN. Second, when there is someone helping them discover just where they are stuck and supporting them to choose the new, to take the risk. We can support the choosing of the new in both of these ways. What an opportunity! We can start with ourselves at step number one, and in doing so become step number two; we also have the privilege of being therapists, with the skills and knowledge to be able to support others in their choices to let go of the past, and to understand that the past does not equal the future.

"The present moment is all you ever have." Really ponder on that. What do you think of it? What if it were true? What would that say about all our worries, concerns, anxieties and drama. Feel into the truth of the idea that you cannot be both unhappy and fully present in the now. What a healing tool! But it is not simply a technique, it is a way of being that requires application and will to achieve. It is maybe one that we never fully master, but small steps make a huge difference. Eckhart Tolle talks about

"Psychological time" which is when you are always trying to get to somewhere other than where you are, that the future is the place to be. Psychological time is also about dwelling on the past, in guilt and blame and regret. He considers this a mental disease, and indeed it is hard to disagree. Much of the work we do as therapists is with dwelling on the past, being unable to let go of past events, worries or unrealistic expectations about the future, perfectionism leading to paralyzing anxiety about future failure. All eliminated by being in the now.

This is certainly something we have to live, or at least practice living, ourselves in order to be able to talk to clients about it. If you truly wish to be authentic you must walk the talk of what you do. Be reflective, make changes where necessary, notice what works and what doesn't, and change what doesn't, address issues which may be holding us back, and be honest and keen in looking for our own blind spots and addressing them. The privilege of therapy is that we can learn from our clients as much as they can learn from us, and they can continue to inspire us to lead a better life and be the best we can be. The wonderful thing here is that being the best we can be as a therapist is fully aligned with being the best we can be as a human—aware, compassionate, wise, joyful, loving, hopeful, humble. Worth it? I'd say so.

It may be too much of a leap for some to simply go straight to acceptance of the past and the events in it, and for these people letting go of the past may include the step of working with forgiveness. Forgiveness is an area that is attracting some attention; in the late 1990s, Stanford University conducted a research project called The Forgiveness Project directed by Fred Luskin PhD. Programs are still run based on the success of this project. They discovered that forgiveness comes with improved social and emotional functioning, reduced anger and decreased anxiety and depression. There are also indications that forgiveness helps improve physical health, producing positive changes in measurements of cardiovascular and nervous system health. It suggests that using forgiveness to help let go of the past can be an effective method of creating more peace and positivity in your life. How we react to hurts is up to us. Forgiveness can increase optimism, hope, compassion and vitality.

Releasing the past exercise

It is helpful to release old patterns and beliefs that prevent you from aligning to your highest purpose. Be grateful for them, and how they have worked for you in the past, and acknowledge that you have outgrown them and no longer need them. Be grateful, and let them go.

Questions to ponder

Where in your life has the past held you back?

Where do you still cling to old ways?

What do you hold on to, that if you let go of it, your world would change?

Where do you feel stuck?

In order to unstick, what do you need to let go of?

Chapter 7

The Tyranny of the mind: learning to come from the heart

There is nothing so disobedient as an undisciplined mind, and there is nothing so obedient as a disciplined mind.
Buddha

Sometimes therapy feels like we are doing constant battle with minds—our own, or our clients'. From monkey mind chatter to unhelpful thoughts, from ruminating to reframing, we focus a lot on the mind, and with good reason. In this era, and in western culture, we revere the mind. We think with enough intelligence we can think our way out of anything. The mind has taken over, and instead of being our servant, has become our master. We have uncontrollable thoughts, irrational thoughts, racing minds and identification with our thoughts. All this thinking has led to a kind of mind primacy in which we forget to use other 'senses' to help us navigate our lives, and make decisions. What has gone most by the wayside is heart based knowing. Some would call heart based knowing intuition or gut instinct, but for me this doesn't go far enough. Listening to the heart is more about following an inner knowing; more than just feeling, we know, but we know through feeling rather than with our heads. Often this inner knowing is completely drowned out by the mind, logic and rationality. We lose our connection with a deeper knowing and tend to go with the loudest, strongest pull, which is the mind. The more we do this, the less we access the heart, and so the pattern goes on.

I don't mean to imply that the mind is not useful. In so many ways our minds have brought us a long way. All of those reading this book will have relied on their minds, often exclusively, to get themselves through college and even life in general. We use our minds to help navigate relationships, make decisions, decide whether we like something or not, and what is right and wrong. Outwardly this seems to have worked well. Many of us mind addicts are apparently successful and functioning in life and society. I would venture to state though, that this is in spite of our mental addiction rather than because of it.

On the other hand, others do not do so well, and when we work with clients it is often their mind that is the biggest obstacle to cure. Those that arrive in our offices suffering from anxiety, depression and inability to make decisions are a case in point, and we find ourselves spending hours trying to help them create strategies to still their mind, notice their mind, or replace their unhelpful thoughts with more helpful ones, depending on your tools of practice.

I have found it difficult to work with clients on stilling the mind when I do not practice it myself, and it is in practicing it, that I can really begin to understand the difficulties and challenges involved.

I have found in working with clients to help them practice stilling their mind, that even the smallest improvement creates a noticeable difference. They feel there is more space in their heads. Their worries and anxieties may still exist but the increased stillness means they are less overwhelmed by these and feel able to manage or co-exist with them. It is as though, in having more space and less self-criticism, they create a greater threshold for self-containment and self-soothing. Decreasing the mental chatter allows people to get in touch with their feelings, which really is what therapy is all about. For me and in my work this is central. Feel what you are feeling, even if you can't label it or name it, or even know if it's 'good' or 'bad.' This is the way to clear right through all issues and no-go zones, so you can imagine how important it is for a therapist to do this themselves given the importance of maintaining a safe, judgment-free zone.

Encouraging the client to feel as they feel is the key to the therapy, and often it starts with numbness, or nothingness. The feeling may have been totally suppressed by the head. Eclipsed by the story, the logic, and the submission to what is considered the right or wrong thing to feel. There is always something under the numbness or non-feeling.

Mindfulness has more of a focus on being rather than doing; this practice brings feelings up much closer to the surface, especially early on in its practice. There may be a bit of an overflow at first after years of suppression. This is okay but the client may need to be reassured, and you are in a far better position to do this if you have been through it yourself.

Beliefs

Beliefs are mental constructs that we use to make sense of the world. They help create meaning. Beliefs are fertile ground in therapy, and our clients can learn a lot about themselves in exploring them. We all have beliefs, some are so strong that they seem part of our identity and we defend them as such. Often the obstacle in therapy that we may at times find ourselves butting heads with can be the clients' beliefs; we may possibly have a clash of beliefs when our own decide to make an appearance. We are all full of beliefs of many different types and beliefs, to state the obvious, are all things we *believe* to be true. Objectively we know that 'beliefs' are different to 'truths', but we lose the knowledge of this difference when the belief belongs to us, because our beliefs are 'true' to us, or we wouldn't believe them. This is why beliefs can be so hard to budge. The best practice in noticing beliefs in others is to practice on ourselves. It is good practice to bring our own beliefs to the surface into our consciousness. When they are conscious we can look at them, and assess which ones we wish to keep, and which we may have outgrown, or are no longer useful. Even if we find ourselves attached to certain beliefs, actually knowing we have a particular belief can help us maintain our neutrality and help us leave our own beliefs and agendas outside the door. I am not suggesting that we become belief free, but it may be liberating to experiment with rephrasing our statements containing beliefs to start with, "I believe that...." This can prove challenging when we really believe something is true, but is really good practice, as it reminds us that it is simply a belief. If we start doing this we are in a much better position to offer this to our clients when we notice how some of their beliefs are getting in the way of progress.

Some beliefs are self-limiting and do not serve. These beliefs can be hard to challenge initially because people tend to find evidence that fits with what they believe and discard or forget what doesn't. They will therefore have a weight of biased evidence to support their belief, making it difficult for them to budge, so when working on beliefs in general it may be useful to challenge those less entrenched beliefs and then move in on the self-limiting beliefs, planting the seed of belief versus truth and seeing where it goes from there.

Challenging self-limiting beliefs creates hope, it highlights that we create our own reality and that if we can choose what we believe why not choose that which supports and encourages us? It is helpful to ask our clients, and often ourselves the question:

Do your beliefs currently support or contradict what you want to achieve?

The inner critic
What other people think of you is none of your business

I'm sure we are all familiar with the critical voice inside our heads which spends quite some time telling us how we'll probably fail, that we are dreadful therapists, that we are stupid or that no one likes us. How banal and childish these words look in black and white. But when they are inside our heads and charged with emotion they can become quite an obstacle to us being and striving to be our best. In some people this voice is so powerful it literally paralyzes them. It interferes with their ability to relate to people, get a job, leave the house and live a meaningful life. This inner critic is often set up with a benign, even loving, intention. We think it helps motivate us, move us forward, or be better. The reality is that it usually ends up being at best, a nuisance, a hindrance to being our best and at worst, a destroyer of our best. It is often set up in childhood with the idea that if we criticize ourselves hard enough no one else will be able to. It can be made worse by being exposed to extremely criticizing influences, but it seems to get set up even without this. This voice is never helpful and is really all about fear of what other people think of us. We imagine all the negative things that could be thought by others about us and then say them to ourselves. At this point the inner critic has got out of our control and some people spend an inordinate amount of time and energy fighting to regain control of their lives. Unfortunately this can be difficult because they have placed a lot of importance and trust in this inner critic; it feels unsafe to let it go. Therapy with someone who is experiencing this can reach an impasse. It can be helpful then not to aim to get rid of the inner critic but to play with the idea of retraining it as a coach. This requires more of a CBT approach. First noticing the thoughts and criticisms then finding a more useful, positive and constructive way to frame them, and working on practicing this. It is often helpful for the client to start to make note of what is said by the critical voice so that they start to become familiar with the usual patterns and strategies it uses, and then to choose other more supportive and helpful coaching styles to work on being their best, as this is where the inner critic's existence came from in the first place. It is also helpful to notice what beliefs support this inner critic and look at dismantling through exploration of alternatives and other CBT type approaches. The inner critic is often set up as a way to let the person know what other people must be thinking of them and to change their actions accordingly.

Heart knowing over mind
Listen to your heart

We believe our mind knows best and can work everything out, in giving this part of us so much power we ignore our other compasses which can give us clues as to what is going on, what our best path would be and what feels right. Logic and rationality can be a tricky process and while it seems to be objective, it is true that we can really rationalize anything. In doing this we often override our instincts or our heart's knowing about the best path. Rationality is not wisdom, and sometimes the wisest choice cannot be rationalized. As we continue to give our mind more and more influence over us the other guidance systems we have get weaker and weaker through disuse. We all know what heart knowing is—we may call it different things, gut instinct, a feeling in my waters, an intuition. Because we prize rationality we do not often follow these feelings if we cannot find a rationale for doing so. We will almost always go with the approach that seems most logical, despite the fact that this often does not work and we find ourselves acknowledging, usually too late, the fact that we 'knew' we should have made the other decision. We can idolize rationality in such a way we become divorced from our own innate knowing and fail to be able to feel our way with any accuracy. We come to rely on mental gymnastics to come to decisions and because of this loss of inner compass, decision making becomes harder and harder leading to paralysis in decision making—an inability to determine for ourselves what the best choice is for us. Part of the problem here is that many of us have lost touch with our heart to the point that we don't even know what we want. Making a decision under these circumstances is of course going to be a roll of the dice.

It comes down again to the idea of accepting where we are and choosing with our heart where we want to be and from there finding our way.

This is a great place to get to with clients, as well as ourselves, as it starts the deconstruction process and begins the journey to the truth.

The value of stilling the mind and coming from the heart

The practice of stilling the mind is one of immense value and as such it is becoming more and more a priority in psychology and counseling with practices such as mindfulness, meditation and ACT being embraced as therapies. Mindfulness seems misnamed as in fact the practice of mindfulness leads to a stilling of the mind and an opening for more feeling and less mind! However, mindfulness is contributing vast amounts to our tool box for ourselves and clients. When we still the mind we start to allow the voice of the heart to be heard. But why come from the heart? What does that mean? Many of us and many of our clients are used to coming from the head. We use our minds for everything. It is like an overused muscle, and the more we use it the weaker our heart knowing 'muscle' gets, and so the less in touch we are with the things we call intuition or gut instinct or feelings. Using the mind is often very appropriate. It is not, however, *always* appropriate. We see daily the difficulties that over-thinking gets people into. Clients that ruminate have obsessive or unhelpful thoughts, hyper-rationalize or get into 'analysis paralysis.' Excessive criticism is an overuse of the mind also, as discussed above, and is commonly seen in practice especially in the form of self-criticism. We can perhaps even recognize when we get into some of these states ourselves.

Take a moment to sit back and be still. Close your eyes, notice your thoughts and your mind's activity. What's going on in there? Sit still and notice your thoughts and consciously let them go. Notice how often they come up and how often your mind is still. Initially you'll probably notice that the mind is rarely, if ever, still. Sometimes there seem to be layers and layers of thoughts. When you think about it, it is amazing that we function as well as we do with such distraction. Imagine how much better it could be without all that excessive chatter! Using the stilling the mind practices set out below, you and your clients will be able to start removing some of the obstacles to coming from the heart caused by excessive, even obsessive thinking.

We have all had a feeling or urge about something, only to rethink it, and find that our initial response was correct. It is important to start trusting our hearts and the knowing which comes from there, and to use our mind as a servant not have it as master. We have deified the mind. We believe that thinking can be infallible and logic and reason are always right. This is a dangerous practice as our minds only know as much as we do, but coming from the heart enables us to access an inner knowing that is eternal, ageless and wise, coming from somewhere greater than us or certainly greater than our little minds. Feel into this yourself and experiment with it, see whether it works for you. As we can see from the above, despite this love affair with our minds, it is clear that they can run away with us. Many of the mental patterns and programs we set up, such as the inner critic, while often set up for good reasons are not fulfilling their purpose, are outgrown and indeed have become destructive.

Stilling the mind allows us to be able to pay attention and maintain our intention to pay attention. Paying attention is an act of will and expresses our care as a therapist for our clients. Loving and non-judgmental attention creates the space of safety and compassion for the client to start to heal. Listening is an important part of paying attention. Undivided attention and focus is a crucial part of the therapy process. Clients need to feel heard, validated, loved and supported within their sessions.

This act of paying attention is difficult and requires a lot of practice. Our minds are busy and undisciplined, and we have days where our own lives get in the way. We may be unwell, worried, overworked, anxious or going through our own process. This necessarily must be left behind at the beginning of the workday to be picked up again, if you still want it, at the end. Stilling the mind practices, strong will and determination as well as discipline are so important here, or else the healing tool we are providing for clients' use is not really useful or effective. This profession is a privileged one. Our job is to help people, or provide the tools for them to move forward, and help themselves should they so choose. We are privileged to enter their private worlds and given their trust. It is important that we place great value on this and in return give the best value we can back to the client. If we do less than this we are not doing this sacred work adequately.

Identification with the mind gives it more energy; observation of the mind withdraws energy from it. If the mind is being observed then the question arises — what is observing the mind? This is like a higher self, one that does not get caught up in emotional triggers, fear, anxiety and drama. This is the great value of mindful awareness. If we practice observing ourselves and the mind and do this all the time, we can no longer be completely caught up in the turmoil and tempest of the mind and thoughts and the emotions they trigger. Some of us can, but the rest is simply observing. Immediately there is a consciousness of our bigger being.

Stilling the mind exercises

There are many ways to work on stilling the mind. You may wish to purchase a meditation CD or go to meditation or mindfulness classes. If you would like to try some exercises without doing this, here are some below.

Breathing

Sit in a chair with your feet flat on the floor and your back straight. Close your eyes and breathe in through your nose. Focus on your breathing and notice the feeling of the air coming in and out of your nose. If you find it difficult to keep your focus there you can count your breaths or use the words "in" "out" as you breathe. When you notice your mind chattering or thinking, just notice that, let go of the thoughts and return to the breath and refocus. It doesn't matter how often you need to do this, just keep doing it. The mind can take some time to become more disciplined. Aim to spend 10 minutes per day doing this initially.

Meditation with a candle

Sit in a chair with your feet flat on the floor and have a lighted candle in front of you that you can focus on. Keep your gaze on the candle and keep your focus there. As in the above exercise, if you notice your mind wandering, let go of the thoughts and bring your focus back to the candle.

If you choose to, you can use the above ways of stilling the mind to enable you to access some of your feelings. As the mind feels stilled, allow the feelings to come up, whatever is there, and explore them. It is common to feel 'nothing' that's okay. Let yourself feel into the nothingness. If there is numbness, allow yourself to explore what's under it. Feel what there is to feel—if there is nothing to feel, feel the nothing. Just for this time suspend the sense of good and bad, should and shouldn't. Avoid engaging in the 'story' of your feeling, why it is there and what happened to you to cause it. Just simply explore and feel the feeling. Be curious about the feelings. Not the story, simply the feeling.

Chapter 8

Compassion in therapy – it all just is

The highest form of wisdom is Kindness.
Talmud

So much is being written at the moment about the importance of compassion in human life. Neuroscientists are measuring it, spiritual leaders are talking about it, and psychologists are writing about it and exploring it in their therapy. I was recently at a large conference, attended by many scientists and psychologists, where much of the discussion was around compassion and empathy and what it means to be human. It seems that science is newly discovering wisdom as old as time. To be happy we need compassion, to be shown it and to show it. But what is it and why is it important in therapy?

Compassion is a space of non-judgment, of understanding that things are as they are, and that it is perfect that way. As all of those in practice can attest to, things only move in therapy when the client feels safe and trusts us. True compassion elicits this trust as surely as judgment breaks it. Compassion comes when we see that all events and phenomena in our lives are opportunities for learning and growth, so that when we see these events in others' lives we do not judge them but see them as an opening of possibility. We can really only attain this if this is how we choose to see our own lives. If we live this way then this attitude would be implicit in the way we work; the lack of judgment and openness we exhibit transfers itself as a possibility to the client rather than the explicit statement or the reframing of the perceived disaster as a blessing—another sure way to lose someone!

Many things are useful in therapy: listening, the focus on

the person, the skilled questioning, even at times, the direction that may be offered. But these things don't go very far without compassion. Compassion is the key to true transformation of self, and through self, others.

Compassion in therapy grants space to the client to see themselves and their lives in other ways. It may enable them to feel gratitude—another important key that we will discuss further and which is a quality now well known in psychology as a healing factor for depression and anxiety. It may enable them to see other options, or even move into a feeling of acceptance for how they are, rather than fighting their reality. Compassion generates compassion in others, and so the healing cycle begins, as compassion encompasses so many qualities—wisdom, love, acceptance, gratitude and joy.

What is compassion? Words that spring to mind to help get a feeling for it are warm heartedness, understanding, wisdom, love. Compassion is about recognizing the sameness of all that we are. It is about recognizing that we all suffer and we all want to be happy, that we are all on the same journey, it is also about recognizing that we cannot always see the big picture and make sense of events, so that to judge them is pointless. Compassion starts with allowance and acceptance—allowing things to be as they are. When you think about it, it is obvious we have little control over that, yet how often we fight it. Practicing allowance and acceptance allows a kind of flow where enough space opens up for us to explore where we are, how we got there and where we would like to be without judgment on the present. Denying, ignoring or fighting our current situation is the surest way to get, and stay, stuck there.

Sometimes our suffering can be our best teacher and provide us with gifts that we often may only recognize in retrospect, or if we are in deep judgment, never at all. To be in compassion we must be open to the learning that is the gift in all that befalls us, both 'good' and 'bad' and to release the judgment we place on people and events. Compassion is about acknowledging our sameness as humans and seeing that all the differences we note, young, old, rich poor, educated, uneducated, kind or cruel, are all superficial. Those people we judge most are our best teachers of compassion as when we feel compassion for them we learn to love the unlovable, which is the basis for our own journey of self-compassion and self-acceptance. For our clients, it creates an amazing space of love and acceptance that they may then be able to make use of in their own progress on their journey. Another's judgment may keep them as stuck as their own; to have a space where they are free to be as they are creates the possibility for change, should they so choose. Compassionate people are harmony seekers, recognizing the oneness of all people, melting down divisiveness and artificially created often mental segregation. Compassion in practice abolishes the delusion of separation that most of us hold as truth. The more compassion we show, and are able to teach and engender in others, the more harmony and unity is created on the planet, and so the more peace—and that could never be a bad thing!

When you are in compassion as a therapist you can feel with another person, but unlike sympathy, and even empathy, you are able not to buy into those feelings or identify with them as though they were your own. Feeling compassion requires being able to feel all this and yet be able to maintain one's own space and boundaries. As well as helping to generate unity and harmony, compassion helps to create understanding and acceptance. Compassion helps to generate hope and the possibility to heal. Along with holding a compassionate space for our clients, we must also nurture the seeds of compassion in them. Part of this is holding that space and teaching by example. It is also about teaching explicitly the ideas and precepts, and, don't forget, the *benefits* of compassion. As compassion for others and compassion for self exist together, clients will experience increased happiness, joy and unity. In addition they will feel a decrease in anger, resentment, guilt and self-loathing. By helping to develop a client's true compassion for self, compassion will expand out and encompass others, as will self-love. Compassion for others also helps to put our own pain and suffering in perspective and may decrease the anxiety and rumination that may accompany excessive attention and worry about self. Whether or not the practice of compassion helps others, we know without doubt that the benefits of it are immense for the person practicing it, which means that in helping our clients achieve compassion we are working towards their highest good and benefit. In doing so we are also working towards the highest good for humanity and our civilizations.

It is important to remember to practice compassion for all beings, rather than simply for the client. A client may come to you as the victim of cruelty by others, torture, rape, abuse or other acts of cruelty and hate. It is easy for us to feel compassion in this circumstance for the victim, and this is wonderful, but if we do not feel equal compassion for the perpetrator of the act then our compassion is not whole. It is biased and based on our judgment. This increases hate and judgment in the world, as well as division, rather than decreasing it. This kind of situation is an opportunity to practice the rather high-level skill I mentioned earlier—loving the unlovable. Loving the unlovable does not mean that we think acts of cruelty and hate are desirable, but simply that we remove our judgment (which in fact achieves very little other than making us feel self-righteous and 'good'), accept what has happened, exercise compassion and do what we can to stop these kinds of acts, usually by nurturing kindness and compassion in all those we meet. This is not about thinking that it is okay to hate and hurt people, but is about taking a positive approach to changing our world, rather than adding to the hate, judgment and negativity. This is not a pacifist argument. There are certainly times where it is absolutely right to fight, even with violence, for ethics and truth. It comes down to the intention.

Are we fighting a war to show we are the biggest and best, to show that our way is the right way, or are we fighting a war to right a wrong, to release the oppressed and to make the world a better place? Compassion is not a weak wishy-washy feeling. It is a quality of great strength that may even co-exist with war. Compassion is not about making excuses for people and why they behave the way they do. It is purely about raising ourselves and the world to a higher level of wisdom, understanding and love.

I have mentioned that part of compassion is the understanding that all humans suffer and that we all want to be happy. We chase happiness all kinds of ways and with all kinds of methods. We believe money will make us happier, yet we have never been richer, and apparently have never been more unhappy! So what's going on here? Most people believe that to be happy you cannot feel sad, or angry, or frustrated, or frightened, or any other perceived negative emotion. To be happy, we seem to believe, requires a one-dimensional emotional experience. Just happiness. This then leads to a sense of failure when we feel a perceived negative emotion which we quickly rush to suppress by trying to make ourselves happy again, usually through an external process such as acquiring something. But all other emotions are compatible with happiness as happiness is freedom from judgment, the exercise of compassion and acceptance of all events and emotions as experiences on our journey. Any happiness we create which relies on something external to ourselves can be removed from us as it relies on external factors, such as a new car or a new boyfriend, a holiday, or even having a baby. But if happiness occurs due to how we are in the world, for example, cultivating compassion and kindness, this happiness cannot be taken away. Unhappiness is the same. We may feel unhappy due to external stimulation, such as sad events or losing things we are attached to, but if we have cultivated happiness within us, due to how we are, we remain happy but simply having a response to a sad event. An understanding of this can really help people get a perspective on how they are feeling and how their chasing of happiness is affecting them, and perhaps allow them to find other ways to achieve a truer and lasting happiness through compassion.

Questions to ponder

Are you helping to end suffering?

How can you be more compassionate in your life?

When someone shows you compassion, how does this feel?

When you experience compassion from another, how does this move and inspire you?

Chapter 9

When it doesn't work – and burnout

Doing one's duty, however small, in an unattached manner gives rise to the awakening of self-awareness.
Sri Sathya Sai Baba

We often hear these days about 'compassion fatigue.' I believe this phenomenon is incorrectly named. True compassion does not get fatigued. What is called compassion fatigue is the use of, and then exhaustion of, sympathy, or even of empathy, which though far preferable to sympathy is still aimed at relieving the distress of the other, often because we feel that distress ourselves as though it were our own. The aim to relieve the distress has an agenda and, indeed, a judgment implied.

Compassion is a complete absence of judgment. It is a wisdom and acceptance that each is on their own journey, that we all wish to avoid suffering, and that sometimes suffering happens. Compassion is not about fixing people, judging their suffering, trying to make them feel better or identifying with the suffering as though it were your own. These things, which are not compassion, are fatiguing.

When using sympathy in trying to help others we come from a place of fear and judgment, we judge that what they are going through is dreadful and that we would not want to be there, that we should help, that things need to be fixed. It is an idea that something has gone wrong. Over time this becomes overwhelming. There is too much going wrong, too much to fix, and it can be so hard to help in any meaningful way and have an impact on the suffering of others. This leads to fatigue and burnout. It is caused by a feeling of helplessness or inability to help. This is a point often made in psychological literature—

73

that people are more likely to help if they feel that their help is capable of succeeding and that they have something to offer.

The difference between sympathy, and even empathy, and compassion feels like this to me. Sympathy is about drawing on my own personal resources to help someone and using sympathy, I would try to help others according to my own ideas of what is best for them and the situation. I only have my own experiences, knowledge and energy to draw on for this and these are all finite. Compassion on the other hand is like drawing from an eternal wellspring of wisdom and acceptance, a knowledge that I cannot know everything and that I am no judge of what is 'good' and 'bad' according to my own pea brain. Compassion is about knowing that you don't know the full meaning and repercussions of experiences; it is about not judging, and yet also understanding the suffering of the other without claiming it as your own, or feeling it as if your own, but also full acknowledgement of it. Compassion aims to relieve the suffering of others, *without attachment*, and for the highest good of all concerned. Empathy and sympathy are attached to relieving suffering as we identify ourselves with it, which makes it painful for us; we judge it as bad, unfair, and needing to be changed or stopped.

When we try to alleviate the suffering we perceive in other people, with the idea that we have failed if we don't, it is easy to feel hopeless or indeed unappreciated. We can feel that we are putting in the hugest effort for no reward, with no appreciation.

Descriptions of burnout are different in the literature. They include terms such as fatigue, disengagement, hopelessness, helplessness, emotional exhaustion and emotional drain. Key components of burnout are profound weariness and 'complete depletion of the self'. It is obvious that we can become so depleted if we use our own personal energy reserves, sympathy and limited perception to try to help people. The more of an agenda we have and the more we have an idea of what would be most helpful, the more we run the risk of depleting ourselves.

'Knowing' how people feel and what they might be thinking is a part of empathy, even compassion. But it is not enough. There is no caring here. Feeling as other people feel is helpful in that it gives us an insight into their world, but the problem with this kind of empathy is that there is no differentiation between that person and us. We feel their emotions as though they are our own and it is this way that burnout lies. It is also more helpful for our clients if there is some level of detachment. We do not want to be sobbing in session along with our clients. We need to maintain a space of hope and compassion for them.

We have to be careful that this detachment does not lead to, and is not equated with, indifference. It is important to be able to feel how the client is feeling, but not as if we were the client. We need to be able to differentiate between our own experiences and others'; to understand their suffering but not claim it as our own. This can be a difficult difference to understand. It is not coldness and detachment, though it may be seen as such by some. It is that we create our own anchor and feel from ourselves without subsuming ourselves in the other. We must maintain our own self-awareness, and our boundaries, at all times and be aware of the difference.

As usual, it all comes back to the self. Compassion must start with the self. We cannot feel compassion for others without feeling it also for ourselves. It is important to practice this, notice where we are judging ourselves, or applying different standards to ourselves, because we think we should be stronger or smarter, or somehow further along the path than our clients. If we come from a true place of equality with our clients, we truly give them value. The method of teaching and leading clients along a path from the front is outdated. It is not about teaching anymore, it is about being. It is okay that they are going where perhaps we haven't been. What is important is that we pay close attention to our own growth and development and put into practice in our own lives what we practice in the therapy room, and what we hope our clients will practice. Otherwise we will be leading from behind — only possible if we are going backwards which, really, is not at all the aim.

Burnout can also occur when we start to feel deskilled, perhaps working with difficult clients or without much support. We can start to feel we are not able to do the job we are being asked to do, and we may become critical of ourselves, lose confidence and even become avoidant about supports we may have in place such as supervision. Part of avoiding burnout is working towards removing the judgment on what we consider to be failure in therapy. As counselors and psychologists we have the opportunity to learn and grow from therapy 'failure'; those times we simply make no progress with a client such as when we do more and more work and nothing happens for them, when we then decide that we are doing too much work and let go, and still nothing happens for them. The relationship is rocky, the rapport patchy. In situations like this I have spent a lot of time wondering what I am doing wrong, wondering whether I know how to do my job and whether the service I offer is value for money. I feel like a failure, or less dramatically, I feel like my work with this particular client is a failure. If I continue with this viewpoint, especially when working with difficult clients, I run the risk of going down the burnout route. 'Failure', though, can be such a rich area for growth and development. Learning to accept failure, and learn from it, even to be grateful for it and for the opportunity it presents to acknowledge our feelings, anxieties and self-worth is vastly valuable when working in counseling. When I was a student retraining after having already spent some years in a counseling role, I suspected I was the only one who had these worries that I somehow couldn't do what all other therapists could do, that I was somehow a fraud, or not a 'real' therapist. During this training I was exposed to literature that discussed therapy failure. Imagine my surprise and relief when

I discovered that some of the most well-respected therapists had times where they wished they were a waiter (Boscolo) or, "converted to religion and prayed for a real therapist to walk in the door" (Flaskas). This really opened up an entirely new space for me, to know this was normal and that it was still possible to be a good and even excellent therapist and have these feelings and doubts. That in fact these feelings and failures were all opportunities to learn more and to constantly find better ways to do things.

Psychotherapy is simply a tool that a person may make use of to the degree they wish. It may be that no matter how good the therapist is, how clear, how loving and attentive, the person may not make use of it or alternatively, a person may cure themselves without therapy at all. Peck discusses this and calls it the will to grow and says it is a crucial determinant in the success of therapy.

Becoming a great, intuitive, experienced and effective therapist takes years of practice. We are constantly learning, changing, and adapting, and continually finding better ways to work with and support clients. This is the most amazing opportunity for growth and development. The cost of gaining this growth and experience, though, is the undergoing of a series of humiliations, or that which we see as humiliation. Such things as therapy failure, clients who don't come back, trials of new ideas and ways of working which don't work, discoveries of our own massive blindspots and triggers that we weren't aware of. These are the gifts of experience to us and if we are robust and resilient enough, and if we have the strength courage and determination to continue, all these can contribute to our development into wonderful and skilled therapists.

Preventing burnout

In trying to prevent burnout, we must keep in mind the value of holding compassion for those we work with and remembering to release all judgment on them, their situation and their pain. Practice compassion in your work and notice when you feel drawn in or in judgment. Practice working with acceptance and hold that together with the desire to change.

It is of great importance to keep up supervision and peer consultation as sometimes we have such great expectations of ourselves that we are destined for disappointment and discouragement. Supervision helps keep things real, while ongoing professional conversations with peers reminds us that we all have difficult times and clients that we feel we cannot help, or who even seem to get worse.

As counselors we are used to being in the role of helper and giver. Make time to practice being a receiver in your life as well; notice how easy or difficult this is for you. If it is difficult, keep practicing. Give the giving a break, to replenish and appreciate yourself and allow others to appreciate you. You'll come back all the stronger and better for it. Remember also to acknowledge the other roles you have in your life of friend, parent, child, lover fitness freak, traveler or whatever else you are. Love and take time to give energy to these so that they are not subsumed and then taken over by your role as counselor and helper/healer.

Use the self-esteem practices in this book to work on having a sense of self-worth that does not come from external things such as how good you are at your job, or what others think of you, but comes from inside yourself so it can remain steady and strong throughout whatever comes along.

The other really important practice in this book, a basic to preventing burnout, is to use the energetic hygiene practices of cutting cords and holding boundaries, so that you are able to maintain a steady level of energy without giving it away, depleting it or feeling drained and exhausted during and after work.

Finally, allow clients to be accountable. We all know that how far they are able to progress is up to them and where they feel ready to go, but it seems that we often forget this and blame ourselves if we hit a dead end or a road block in treatment. A client's learning and progress is up to them, and it is up to us to do the best we can for them, and to go as far as they want to go. These are their choices. Their avoidance and denial is not our fault, though it may often be good practice to bring it onto the table for discussion. It is not, however, up to us to force a way through it. Remember, the client does the work. If you find that you are doing all the work, pull back. It's a pretty good sign that you are giving up a lot of your own energy. Understanding that we don't need to have all the answers and that the client is responsible for their progress in therapy, frees us up to be the best counselors we can be, without agenda and with respect for the client.

Keep clear what your reasons are for working in this field and understand what meaning you attribute to it. Find again your joy in practice, what makes you love your job? For me, I am grateful everyday for the joy I find in working with adolescents. I find them inspiring, courageous and straight talking; I appreciate the privilege I have in being able to work with them, gain their trust and be of service to this new generation.

For us to avoid burnout, we must feel we are useful and that our work has meaning. This is why we entered the profession in the first place and so it is important to feel you are still on track. Use the questions in Chapter One to guide your work and direction, so that you feel in alignment with your purpose and so that you know and feel you are determining your own path according to your own values. This and compassion are the most effective preventatives of burnout.

Chapter 10

The power of gratitude and acceptance

At times our own light goes out and is rekindled by a spark from another person. Each of us has cause to think with deep gratitude of those who have lighted the flame within us.
Albert Schweitzer

Gratitude is a transformational energy. It allows us to transform how we feel and what we perceive. It changes our outlook, and allows us to align ourselves towards the positive, towards optimism and joy, as we embrace all of life.

It is important to recognize that things that go well in our lives are as real as those that do not. What we feel good about is as worthy of rumination as that which we feel bad about. The choice then is where we choose to spend our energy and time. Do you choose to focus on that which improves your mood, or that which does not? Imagine you are at a restaurant and have the entire menu choice before you. Would you choose a menu item that you disliked? No, surely not. Most people, indeed everyone I know, tends to go for what sounds to them the most delicious or enjoyable option. So why would we do it any other way with choosing our focus? Put this way it sounds ridiculous, yet this is what we often do when we make choices about what to focus on.

Positive psychology has a big focus on gratitude and teaches that gratitude and optimism can be learned. Feeling gratitude deliberately is all about choosing our focus. It is about choosing what we pay attention to in our lives, because what we pay attention to becomes our story, it becomes our perception, our world view. The great thing here is that if you don't like your world view, it looks like you can change it!

The importance of gratitude is very well known now with the

recent advent of positive psychology in the field and the interest in the pursuit of happiness. Neuroscientists have measured the effects of gratitude on the brain and its neurotransmitters and have found empirical evidence of what we already know intuitively, that is that gratitude makes us feel good! Other studies show that gratitude boosts our immune system, and can lead to a long term improvement in mood, even permanent if we keep up the gratitude. So let's capitalize on this and expand our ideas of what gratitude is and when to feel it.

What is gratitude? Gratitude is thankfulness, a sense of rightness and of well-being in our existence, a swelling of the heart in appreciation. Acceptance makes up a large part of gratitude and because of this, gratitude cannot co-exist with judgment. If we feel truly grateful for an event we stop judging it. This simple fact goes a long way towards explaining why exactly it is that gratitude makes us happier. Judgment keeps us stuck. When we judge something as wrong we can play it over and over. We become a victim. The sense of unfairness and the time we can spend ruminating on how things should be different prevents us moving on. We know this. Letting go of the past can often form the basis of our work in therapy and we often see this kind of stuckness in our clients and in ourselves if truth be told. Gratitude is a transformational energy that allows us to move on in our lives and also transforms how we see, appreciate and respond in our lives.

Typically we feel gratitude when events or feelings occur which we deem positive. We get a promotion or a great new job, are able to buy the house we like or want or get over a serious illness. We could also be grateful for gifts or other people's acts of kindness towards us. Now let's for one minute adopt the 'Pollyanna' approach. If you read the book, you will know that Pollyanna played a game where she practiced being grateful for things that one would not normally feel grateful for, and finding a reason for it, for example, as a small child she was given a pair of crutches for Christmas when she wanted a doll, but in abiding by the rules of her game she was able to be grateful she didn't need them. Yes it's a bit cheesy I know, but let's take the lesson out of it. If we practice gratitude we can be happier—so why not try and encourage all the gratitude we can, as much as we can, and be inventive about why we are grateful?

Tough circumstances can be valuable, and our 'enemies' can bring us great gifts. Tough situations make us deal with reality, it forces us to step out of avoidance and denial, and really strive to do our best. Under these circumstances we often grow and become wiser, more compassionate, and develop greater understanding. We often hear of people developing a life-threatening or fatal illness such as cancer and expressing that they have changed, become, as they see it "better people" and feeling that they have just learned how to live. Despite being very ill, they often say that the illness was the best thing that ever happened to them. Petrea King says of her experience with cancer that, "in preparing as fully as possible for my own death I discovered a profound connection to life" (p. 19). Your life matters.

Gratitude for things we wouldn't usually expect to feel gratitude for, things that we have felt are wrong or bad, helps us release the judgment and the pain associated with the feelings. Pain, heaviness and that stuck feeling are all clues that we have judgment on something. Feeling gratitude to whatever it is we have judged releases all this. It is not about being unrealistic or naive, for we can certainly discern that not all events and feelings are beneficial, or constitute the quickest path to spiritual growth and happiness, but nevertheless, all events and paths produce learning and growth if we allow it, and that is certainly something to be grateful for. Also, if we know gratitude makes us feel better why not do it? Sometimes we can integrate these ideas into therapy by working with more obvious sources of gratitude and then start looking for things to be grateful for in circumstances that may not be so obvious. Like so many things, feeling gratitude can be a matter of habit. We often work with clients in refocusing their attention onto the more positive things in their life by using gratitude logs and expert questioning. Once this starts coming more naturally to them it is not so great a step to feel grateful for embarrassing moments (what did I learn?), or rudeness in people. (I got a chance to practice maintaining my equanimity and I did really well.)

If it seems impossible to feel gratitude, that indicates that there is judgment attached to the event. Invoking the feeling of gratitude and then applying it to the situation you are feeling stuck over can work, or you may need to actively work on releasing the judgment. This may involve spending a couple of minutes with the eyes closed, visualizing holding something heavy, representing the judgment, and then allowing yourself to let it go, put it down. Letting go of judgment can feel like you are letting someone or something off the hook, but really what you're doing is letting yourself off the hook. We know that judgment keeps you stuck, and we know that with judgment you cannot feel gratitude and acceptance. Gratitude and acceptance substantially increase your levels of happiness, so remaining stuck in judgment knowing all this starts to seem quite self-destructive.

Dropping the judgment is like forgiving someone. Holding a grudge or a judgment is a heavy burden to bear, mainly because it precludes joy, and especially because it prevents people moving on. As long as people bear a grudge or hold a judgment they will ruminate over it reliving the event and cementing the problem. A grudge does nothing more than punish its bearer and yet ironically, the hardest part of letting go is the commonly held perception that not holding a grudge or a judgment means that whatever happened was okay. But really, how is your judgment, and subsequent unhappiness, punishing them? The relief when you drop all that is substantial. Suddenly there is room for hope, joy and love and there is the ability to move forward and live a life worth living. Ideally in the end the forgiveness step may not even be needed. Once you practice and get used to it you can be in gratitude and acceptance all the time, so there is no judgment and therefore no need for forgiveness.

A big clue that we are not in acceptance is when we are fighting or struggling or feeling stuck. Use these situations to practice acceptance. It will make a big difference to your practice.

Gratitude helps to build self-esteem. When people make a real attempt at a gratitude journal or finding things to be grateful for they feel connected, loved and cared for. They notice the kindness of strangers and even feel looked after by luck, or 'higher powers'.

It is interesting that it is only recently that we can talk about these subjects with any great seriousness and in any depth. Before scientists were interested, and when these things were un-measurable, they were not seen as important conversations to have. Now we know that these issues are of utmost importance in human development and evolution. How did we, as a society, develop this view, that all the talk about emotions and qualities, love and compassion is not real gritty stuff to talk about? Instead we seemed, and some still do, to take more seriously the complainers and the cynics. Those who criticize and pick things apart tend to be seen as more intelligent. How does this affect us and how we see the world? It is like we are trained to see the negative, to hide our feelings and those moments when our heart swells within us from compassion or gratitude or hope. We hide it, yet we all have access to and experience of these feelings, and know that they can lead to profound joy and change. So instead of hiding them, let's embrace and encourage them, and encourage our clients to do the same thing. This is how we learn to trust and listen to our own inner guidance rather than critical voices, the decisions of others or the tyranny of the mind. The results speak for themselves.

Gratitude exercises

1. Practice being grateful by keeping a gratitude log. We all know about them and most of us will have worked with clients who are using them, but have you tried it yourself? Gratitude transforms your perception of events and melts judgment away allowing you to learn and grow from the experience.

You can make it a bit more taxing by looking at perceived negative events and finding ways to be grateful for those, see below.

2. When you noticed you are triggered or bothered by something, practice calling in the feeling of gratitude. Is there something about the situation or feeling you can be grateful for? Is it an opportunity to learn? To know yourself more? To feel alive? To feel anything at all? Perhaps simply the opportunity to practice feeling gratitude. See how it works. See it as an opportunity to experiment. Practicing this kind of gratitude work and learning to love the unlovable really illustrates that we do choose our own reality and our responses to events and people in our lives.

Chapter 11

Hanging on to hope

If you lose hope, somehow you lose the vitality that keeps life moving, you lose that courage to be, that quality that helps you go on in spite of it all. And so today I still have a dream.
Martin Luther King

As counselors and psychologists we deal in hope. It is our daily currency, and a major agent of change. Hope is the key to overcoming the problems and obstacles we face in life. The story of Pandora's box illustrates this idea. In ancient Greek Mythology, Pandora, daughter of Zeus was given a box by her father and told not to open it. Of course, curiosity got the better of her, as her father had planned, she opened the box, thus letting escape all the evils known to humankind, including famine, envy, pestilence, and disease. The last thing to fly out of the box, the antidote and weapon against all those things, was hope.

To truly understand how important hope is, imagine not having any. How could we make change? From where would we derive our motivation? How would we be able to persevere? Without hope we are unable to move forward, unable to picture other ways, other ideas; a time when things will be better. When we can't do this we have nothing to move towards. Hope negates despair. It allows people otherwise going through hell to have a glimmer that it may not always be this way, and to allow them simply the idea that they will get through it enabling them to have trust that at some point they will be okay.

Hope is a basic in counseling. The hopeful thing is that in most cases the fact that someone has even showed up for a counseling session would imply they hold at least some small amount of hope. It is important to look at the level of hope in the client, see what's there and how to nurture and grow it. As the counselor there will be times that we may need to hold hope for our clients, when they feel unable to hold it themselves. At these times it is of utmost importance that we maintain and keep strong our faith and trust that the client can reclaim their hope and move forward again, and hold that for them. I am sure we have all experienced hopelessness ourselves in relation to a client and their progress or their situation. If we are not careful to keep our cords clear, and our vision steady, we can fall with the client into hopelessness and despair on their account. If this occurs, the therapist may terminate therapy early, feeling that further progress is impossible, or else they may tell the client that they cannot help them, that they need a different person, an expert. The client will also be able to see that the therapist is losing hope and this will usually end in them leaving therapy, and feeling as though they are 'too hard', and further increasing their despair. If we do not hold the hope for our clients when they can't, we have failed them. As we hold hope for them, and as they witness this, often over long months of work, they start to restore their own hope and the healing begins.

Counseling is not about making things all better. Sometimes people may be in difficult situations, impossible dilemmas, or going through terrible emotional pain. It is not up to us to remove this from them, or convince them that what is happening is a good thing. It's okay that it's awful. Humans learn and grow through experience and we have all types of it. Hope is part of what gets us through. Hope that it will get better, that I can feel better, that somehow it will work out for the best, and that I can survive. Hope is what creates possibility and the will to go on. Hope breeds optimism and optimism breeds hope. As therapists we must work with and recognize hope where we find it. Encourage it, nurture it, discuss it, and explore it. Where does the client hold hope? In what aspects of their lives do they feel they have hope, and where are they feeling hopeless? It is important to be real about this and not just look incessantly, and irritatingly at the bright side. It is about holding hope side by side with hopelessness, despair and devastation. It is not as contradictory as it sounds. Pandora's box let out all the challenges and problems in the world, and out with those, at the bottom of the box, came hope, the tool that is gifted to us to help us meet these challenges.

Our level of hopefulness is directly linked to how we perceive the world, because our worldview will have a direct relationship with how we perceive those events and situations that occur to us. An optimistic viewpoint will help support hopefulness. Your experience of life is up to you. You decide your perceptions and worldview. If not you, then who? As this is the case, if you want to become more optimistic, lead a happier, more joyful life and be more hopeful, then changing your perceptions and worldview would be a really good idea.

The reason hope is so useful when working with people is that it helps to create possibility. Hope creates the space to allow the exploration of options and ideas and alternatives. From this perspective we open ourselves up to inspiration and a different perception of events. When we really do hope for the best we send our thoughts into that possibility, and as mentioned before, energy follows thought. In hoping we visualize the outcome we want, we see it happen. We expect there to be a solution, and in so doing we often find one, because we do not give up. It is easy to see why hope is such a healing quality and how helpful, indeed essential, it is to bring it into the therapy room ourselves, and to nurture and encourage it in clients for their best outcome.

To create and nurture hope we need to both explicitly and implicitly bring it into the room. We absolutely must hold hope ourselves for the client and for the results of the counseling. They must be able to feel the hope we hold for them and feel the possibilities open up. It is also good to bring up hope in the sessions, to see how hopeful they feel and let them know that you are hopeful, and to then work on how to increase their hope. The more hope they have, the faster things move in therapy as hope leads to motivation and optimism, which can for many allow them to explore a whole new world of perspectives. As the story of Pandora's box tells us, hope is one of the most valuable tools we can have and use in therapy, and it is extremely worthwhile for us to work on our own experiences of hope to then be able to bring this into the client as part of the work with them.

In therapy we teach our clients to hope by holding hope ourselves. Hope, like fear is contagious. I know what I'd rather catch.

A friend and colleague of mine, Nerida Miles, wrote this:

As Healers and Teachers, we must first and foremost instil hope. This is our responsibility, to instil hope within our patients, clients, within our sphere of influence. This is about the space we hold—as healers, we do not heal anyone, we hold a space of unconditional love and above, we may access, hold and facilitate with regards to our specialities, gifts and abilities, we may facilitate healing energies, yet we do not heal anyone, through the space we hold, instilling hope, another has the opportunity to heal their self. As Healers and Teachers, then, part of the healing space we hold, the energy that we create our next moments with, to even be able to hold a healing space and instil hope for another, we must first hold and instil hope for and within self. We cannot love another anymore then we can love self. Healing is always a two way or two sided experience. If we don't have hope, how, as Healers and Teachers could we instil hope for others and within our sphere of influence?

Questions to Ponder

How important do you see hope in your practice?

How are you able to encourage hope in your clients?
Where are your own strengths and weaknesses regarding hope?
How do you develop hope in your own life?

Chapter 12

Both accepting our feelings *and* choosing our feelings

Between stimulus and response there is a space. In that space is our power to choose our response. In our response lies our growth and our freedom.
Viktor E Frankl

The most important focus in this book is to feel as you feel without judgment. *Feel as you feel without judgment.* Six simple words describing an equally simple way of being. Yes, simple, but hard to achieve, particularly when we make our feelings so complicated we often can't even tell how we feel, let alone feel it without judgment. We spend so much time trying to feel a certain way, striving for happiness or contentment, and feeling inadequate or not good enough when we do not achieve this state. This only adds to our unhappiness, indeed actually causes it. Being able to teach clients to start to practice this way of being is to teach them to transform their own world. Acceptance is a healing balm, and such a relief from the weight of judgment, and the striving to change things that leads to avoidance and denial, a refusal of the reality we are in. All the other practices discussed in this book are about supporting this practice of feeling as you feel without judgment. Gratitude, hope, acceptance, building self-esteem are all steps on the ladder to achieving this state which allows us to be in full mastery of all our levels, spiritual, mental, emotional and physical.

Feelings are different from emotions. Feelings encompass not simply the emotional, but also the physical, mental and spiritual aspects of ourselves. When we check into how we are feeling all of this comes into play. Accepting our feelings is fundamentally important, but does not mean that all and sundry must be at the mercy of our emotions, hearing about them, having them thrown around. Accepting does not mean we must have an outward display of whatever we are feeling as we work through it. Our loved ones' major role is not as the testing ground for our emotional expressions. Acknowledging feelings does not mean that we cannot control them. It may even be appropriate to express them to others as well as ourselves. However, emotions may often be inappropriate, and due to an irrational trigger reaction or unresolved issue, may need to be controlled. We are not entitled to throw our emotions around all over the place simply because we think and have been told that it is bad to suppress them. It is our own responsibility to control them, not by denying and suppressing them and pushing them away, but by noticing them, learning what our triggers are, and clearing them, so that we are the masters of our emotional selves. This is not about rigidity or judgment, but simply emotional maturity.

Accepting emotions and feelings as they are allows them to flow and move, and the acceptance you feel allows you to be free to choose something new. To choose a feeling or state of being that helps you be your best and meet your highest potential in that moment, something that supports you.

Together with accepting our feelings, it is also of great importance to take the responsibility of choosing them. This is not as contradictory as it sounds. The question is, if it is not you who makes the choice, then who? As I discussed in an earlier chapter, to move to where we want to be, we need both to know where we are now and to accept it. If we know where we are the way is clearer to get to where we would prefer to be. If we are unaware of, or fighting the truth of where we are pretending we are somewhere else, we will never be able to navigate. The reason, I think, that accepting seems contradictory to making a change is that many of us see acceptance as resignation, a giving up. Acceptance is not this at all. Acceptance is having a clear perception of how things are with no avoidance and denial. A simple "Here I am." It is only from here that we can ask the next question; "Now what?"

Think again of that metaphor of hiking near a stream, but after some time you realize that it is the wrong stream, definitely not where you want to be and nowhere near the campsite you are aiming for. Now, you have a choice. You can act as though you are at the right stream because you cannot accept that you got it wrong, you can walk up and down for hours looking for the campsite that isn't there, or you can figure out where you are on the map, accept that, even though it may not be ideal and definitely wasn't part of the plan, it is where you are, then work out how to get to the stream from your current position. Our inner world is like this. People, and we may see this in our clients and in ourselves at times if we are honest, often choose to take the first option and deny what they are feeling because they don't want to feel it, or deny their situation because they don't want to be in it. But there it is, whether we like it, or admit it, or not. If we deny what we are feeling we have no awareness of what is really going on and we are unable therefore to take ownership of where we want to be and how to get there. No matter how desperate we are for change, and how hard we work for it, in taking the first option, because we are so desperate for change, we ironically stop being the change agent in our own lives. So, the first step is to accept and the next is to decide "what next?" We cannot move anywhere without acceptance of where we are now.

Acceptance is not resignation, nor is it giving up. It is in fact the only way to move forward and avoid stuckness. Far from being an end point, it is the jumping off point for where we want to go next. We can only captain our own ship from this place of acceptance and clear vision. Acceptance is simply knowing the truth in the moment without delusion. There is always choice from there. You cannot get to where you are going unless you know where you are.

We see this regularly in therapy. Clients are often eager for change, but are unable to move forward because they are stuck in avoidance or denial of their current position and issues. They want to be somewhere different and are judging where they actually are; until they accept where they are now they cannot move. Sometimes this work is the hardest. Clients are often impatient to move forward, to get out of where it is so uncomfortable for them; to stop being anxious, depressed, grieving, angry. When the therapist focuses on the here and now they may feel like therapy is going nowhere. After the acceptance comes, and the judgment is released, movement can be rapid. When therapy feels stuck, using this lens and often explaining the reasoning to the client can be helpful.

Marsha Lineham, creator of Dialectical Behavior Therapy (DBT), now a mainstream therapy used so effectively on some of the most challenging client groups, those with serious suicidal tendencies, cutting and self-harming, often diagnosed as 'borderline', coined the phrase "radical acceptance."

Marsha was hospitalized at the age of 17, and kept in an institution for two years. She was diagnosed with schizophrenia, held in seclusion to stop her ongoing attempts at self-harm, medicated heavily and given electroshock treatments. After being discharged, with little hope from her doctors that she would survive, she made another couple of attempts at suicide, and then one day, while praying, had a revelation.

One night I was kneeling in there, looking up at the cross, and the whole place became gold—and suddenly I felt something coming toward me., It was this shimmering experience, and I just ran back to my room and said, "I love myself." It was the first time I remember talking to myself in the first person. I felt transformed. (New York Times article)

This was her turning point but it took her a number of years and a PhD to understand why, and then she based DBT partly on this simple principle—she had accepted herself. She called this idea 'Radical Acceptance', and paired it with another principle, the need to change. Acceptance of the self and also the need to change. Acceptance in fact *leads to* the ability to change as it releases the judgment that keeps us stuck. This practice is not just for borderline patients at risk of suicide, but can work for all of us.

A lot of energy is spent fighting reality, fighting ourselves, fighting our thoughts and feelings and fighting whatever else we perceive to be wrong with ourselves. Historically, psychology and psychologists joined this fight, to fix people, to change their actions, thoughts and feelings. This has been only partially successful, and has in fact caused a pathologizing of what can be normal human symptoms and reactions to unpleasant or negative events. As the general public became more familiar with psychological thinking they also began to pathologize things, or diagnose themselves, to compare themselves to their perception of others and so find a new platform for the inner critic to hold forth in its wisdom. It has become obvious to many of the new leaders in the field of psychology that a new paradigm is needed.

ACT, along with DBT, is a popular type of therapy that uses acceptance as one of its central tenets. Fighting reality is a waste of time and energy and causes the problem whatever it may be, perhaps chronic pain, anxiety or depression, to interfere with daily life and enjoyment. Acceptance, while seeming counterintuitive, creates room for people to have their 'problem' and live their life without its previous limits. A "both... and..." approach that helps remove what Russ Harris calls the "tyranny of when," the idea that I can only be happy when... I lose weight/ get rid of the pain/become less worried, or whatever the issue is.

Positive psychology has also turned the old paradigm on its head. Psychology used to focus on all that was wrong, symptoms, illness; other negative events. Positive Psychology brings in a whole new approach, focusing on positivity, as well as fostering resilience in the face of adversity. Positive psychology focuses on gratitude, appreciation, hope and optimism. It accepts that 'bad' things happen, but focuses on our perceptions of these events and how that may affect our coping style and ability to respond and recover.

Acceptance is the stepping off point for change. Simple acceptance removes one of the largest obstacles to change, judgment. For this reason it is one of the most important states or qualities to achieve. It is important that we model this for our clients and practice acceptance for ourselves and of ourselves.

Then we can move forward into our new choice.

Making the choice: Psycho-Spiritual qualities.
Acceptance is only the first step. Now is the time to make a conscious choice of change; a choice to choose how to feel and how to be. Because we have this choice, we can choose from the highest level of qualities that we can, the psycho-spiritual qualities.

Choosing other feelings or qualities is not the same as suppressing feelings. Remember we are already in acceptance and our feelings have been acknowledged and accepted. From here we can choose the next step. To be the agent of our own change and to understand that we can actually choose how we feel is extremely powerful. It makes a huge difference for those that have the courage to go there. It is most helpful to choose from a list of the higher psycho-spiritual qualities, such as compassion, love, hope, joy, courage, trust, patience, appreciation and gratitude.

This step is all about taking responsibility for ourselves and making our own choices. It is about moving out of the victim role of the sense of having feelings just happen to us, or events thrust upon us that we feel we have no choice in how to feel about, or how to respond to. We choose all our responses, values and feelings. The freedom in this is huge, but it takes a lot of courage as there is then nowhere to hide.

Acceptance is something all good therapists practice. Just allowing the client to be who they are and how they are, to clarify for themselves what would be most helpful and work with that. If a client sees you are in a state of acceptance and non-judgment, they will feel able to enter this themselves, if only initially in the safety of a session. They may need this encouragement as trying on acceptance is a big step. It involves releasing judgment, guilt and blame, and releasing the story. Before a client takes this step towards vulnerability though, the therapist must demonstrate it themselves, and so there needs to be exploration of what it means, what the obstacles are and what the difference is. To be in acceptance also allows the therapist, and the therapy, to stay in a state of flow as there is no fight against what is happening or judgment on it. It all simply is.

As therapists we make an active attempt to not judge our clients or what they are going through. So how about extending that to people outside the therapy room who are not our clients and, of course, extend it to ourselves, our thoughts, feelings and lives; this work is all about walking the talk. We don't have to be perfect, but we need to be doing what we are suggesting our clients do for a number of reasons. One is so that we learn the pitfalls and difficulties, another is to strengthen the therapeutic relationship as we share the client's journey and another is so the client can witness firsthand how this affects our presence, what we radiate and how we manage our energy. The biggest reason though is for ourselves. Releasing the judgment is integral to helping us move through our issues, maintaining flow in our lives and feelings, and making the most of our growth opportunities.

Judgment in therapy renders it ineffective; judgment in the client about themselves, others or their situation leaves them stuck, as we see often in practice. So it is easy to see how releasing the judgment on our feelings and ourselves could have such a great impact.

Notice emotions, notice feelings, release the judgment on whether they are good or bad, simply accept that you have them and make choices from there.

Acceptance exercises

1. Find a quiet place where you will have at least five minutes uninterrupted. Make sure you are aligned and centered. Now, just allow yourself to be in the present moment. Allow things to be as they are. Allow yourself to be as you are. Be in the stillness of the moment. Allow whatever happens to happen, feelings, emotions, physical sensations, everything. No need to think about it, or name it, just simply a pause from judgment, trying, suppressing, rushing, aiming, attempting and achieving and changing. Just allow. Be in this space for a few minutes and allow yourself to get used to being here.

2. Feel yourself drop the judgment on yourself, on the feeling. Allow that feeling to unstick itself and flow, and see how it changes. Releasing judgment is the key to releasing blocks. Allowing things to be as they are and feelings to be as they are allows all energy to flow/change/release/move/change. Judgment keeps it stuck—stuck to you and stuck to that moment.

Chapter 13

Working with perceptions and loving the truth

Truth is incontrovertible, malice may attack it and ignorance may deride it, but, in the end, there it is.
Sir Winston Churchill

All we see is through our own perception, our lenses. It is the same for our clients. We are not privileged with a better or truer vision simply because we are their therapist. We often just have a different one. By offering our own perceptions, though, and broadening the scope of possibility, we can illustrate the idea that perceptions are just that, perceptions, and that they limit our understanding of the truth. Perceptions get created by our own fears and our own past, leading to a practice of consulting our memories of past events in order to make decisions for the present. This is why many people do the same thing over and over again, even though the results have always been rather less than successful.

Much of what we experience about the 'goodness' or 'badness' of something has to do with our perceptions and our interpretations. These are within our control, and the key to this is losing judgment.

A perception can be the basis of rigid beliefs, and rigid beliefs can cement and create perceptions and we know that people look for evidence to fit their belief system and their perceptions. It is almost as though anything that occurs which does not fit a belief or perception about what is true goes unnoticed and ignored. Anything that does fit is picked up and used to further cement the belief or perception. This would be understandable and even adaptive if we used this ability to cement positive beliefs that made us feel good and helped us to be our best, but it seems that the usual way we do this is to find evidence about negative beliefs, self-imposed limitations. An obvious example of this is the change we see when people start looking for things to be grateful for. What were they looking for before? Usually it was an eye out for negative unpleasant things to fit other less helpful perceptions. Wouldn't it be great to use this amazing filtering ability we all have to support ourselves and help ourselves be bigger, stronger and brighter. We could choose to find evidence to support positive beliefs and perceptions rather than the negative. This at least would be a good start on the way to loving and accepting the truth as it is.

Perceptions can play a big part in therapy too. I am still often surprised by my clients' ideas of how therapy is progressing in comparison with mine, and what they find most helpful and memorable about the sessions. I once worked with an adolescent who was shy and found it difficult to talk, she seemed to find the beginning of the session particularly challenging. I decided, as a warm up, that we would start the session using story cards in which she would pick out a card that had a sentence on it like, "the luckiest day of my life" and talk about it. I decided that since this may be challenging for her, I would do it too, so that we would both be able to tell a story. For me this was simply a way to warm up, so enabling us to get to the 'meat' of the session. For her, at the end of our time together, she remembered those stories, particularly my part in telling my own stories as the most helpful part of her therapy.

Another client seemed to be going dreadfully slowly, and I remember worrying that our sessions were not giving her any value because I couldn't see any progress. When it came to a review of the sessions we had had and a discussion of whether she wanted to continue, she said that despite needing to save up for a special trip she had planned she wanted to spend the money still coming to see me as she had found it helpful. From then I have endeavored to stop making assumptions about how the therapy is going and simply work with the client's experience of this.

The truth is healing and is absolutely necessary for moving forward. Connecting with our hearts, knowing and rediscovering how to recognize the truth, letting go of attachments and ideas are safety mechanisms so we know where we are, who we are. When we can have clear pure intentions, we can live in truth all the time. Truth eliminates confusion, decision making problems and double binds. In order to get to the truth we need courage and we need to want it. It will often involve dismantling all our creations of who we are, our personas, our sense of self. It may mean that we feel we cease to exist, but that is simply an ego state. Really, truth is there anyway, it's just about either acknowledging it or hiding our heads in the sand. If you've ever seen an ostrich do that, you'll know it looks pretty silly from the outside. This truth finding and truth acknowledging is a big job, and certainly a lifelong ongoing process. It is what is meant when people say they break themselves down, and then get to know themselves and the world. Nothing is really broken down except that which is not real, though when we live in a world of illusion that feels like just about everything. We interact with each other through a series of perceptions and illusions, some that are uniquely ours, and some that we all share, matrix style.

As we already know, perceptions and illusions are something we create for ourselves. So, they can be uncreated. With clients, we do this regularly, but often create new perceptions for them to try on. We talk about replacing thoughts with more helpful thoughts, or beliefs with more helpful beliefs. This is a great start, and helps to create the strength and resilience that is needed in the long term to start breaking down all illusion and attachment, but it is important to be aware there is more, and to find the truth and be open to it is the true freedom. As we work with ourselves and with others and break down beliefs and perceptions, this helps to create the awareness that they are not incontrovertible truths. When a client has broken down a number of perceptions in therapy they become far less attached to perceptions in general, and it is far easier for them to see that beliefs they have may not be true. It is this way that we can come to a place where it is possible to let go all beliefs and perceptions, to simply be with the truth.

We must set the intention to want the truth above all things and then really set in to belief busting.

Avoidance and denial

Most or all of the time we are in some state of avoidance and denial. By the time we get to an age where we start to have some insight into ourselves and a desire to know more, be more, feel more, and notice that feeling of searching that most of us are familiar with, we are so loaded up with avoidance and denial we hardly know who we are. I think this may be what is behind the idea people have of 'finding themselves'. They are lost in illusion, and their own created selves, and have lost touch with what the truth is. Somewhere inside us we know that something isn't right, that simply causes us to cover up more, in fear of our own innate defectiveness, when that feeling simply was about avoidance and denial. The last thing needed is more of that! We don't realize that it is us, the real self that has been covered over by a whole lot of rubbish that we created to hide ourselves. I wonder if that is the symbolism of the Adam and Eve story where they decided to cover themselves with fig leaves. They became ashamed of their real selves and created masks and mystery, and started hiding. Perhaps. Anyway whether or not that is the case, it is certainly true that we have been hiding ever since, creating as much armor as we can to cover our soft spots and vulnerability and trying to be what we think others want to see. It is no wonder that some get completely lost in all this.

Avoidance and denial are causes of many of the issues we

see in therapy— covering and suppressing feelings, judgment of being somehow not good enough or wrong, creating impossible standards to live up to or else the refusal to meet any part of one's potential. Letting go of this is brave work and often happens slowly, but little by little we can start to come to our senses.

Being authentic: The professional/private split

We've all had the experience of meeting clients outside of the therapy room, perhaps in the supermarket, at the gym, in a restaurant or even on a holiday. It can seem like two alternate universes colliding. Some therapists feel really uncomfortable in this situation. If this is you, it may be helpful to consider whether this discomfort is pointing to the possibility that who you are as a therapist may not necessarily be congruent with who you are as a private citizen. This split is a great thing to get rid of so that there is no clash of worlds. I am not suggesting that there is no need for privacy, but the fact is these accidental meetings with clients occur in public places where we are happy to be seen by strangers or acquaintances. So why so difficult with clients?

For some therapists, they feel that they need to remain almost two dimensional to their clients, almost as though they have no other life, no messy human existence. Part of the uncomfortable feeling when meeting a client in the shopping center is perhaps that they have seen you out of professional mode, perhaps with your partner or children, perhaps dressed casually or may even have been able to see what you have in your shopping trolley. There can be an uncomfortable feeling that too much information is suddenly leaked. Healing this is important. If we are fully in integrity about who we are, and we are real in sessions, then there is no need to be concerned when we are spotted by clients. We are still ourselves and there is no clash of identity or need to hide our 'true selves'. How freeing not to have to maintain this split.

Being real by losing the professional/private split and just being as we are in all moments enables us to lose our mask in therapy. This helps us keep the therapy and the client real. Sometimes you may have experienced clients affecting a cure that is too quick, too easy. Often these clients are trying to please us as the authority. They want to be good clients and believe that if they don't get better there is something even worse wrong with them than the original presenting problem This can happen regardless of the kind of persona we project as their counselor, but is far more likely to happen if we project a very expert all-knowing grandness that may not fit with who we actually are. This type of persona perpetuates the idea that the counselor is there to cure the client while the patient is only a passive player in this process. The client then gives away all autonomy and self-determination and waits to be cured. This cure is a false one. It doesn't last and may lead to a great loss of confidence on the part of the client. True progress requires hard work by the client and honesty and authenticity in the therapist. It is important that the therapist, while still maintaining a safe space, does not know all the answers and allows the client to be the expert in the room, as well as the player who decides how to use the tool of psychotherapy for their own best fit. Being honest in this way with the client, as well as acknowledging them as a self-determining human being, helps to create trust and confidence. This may be harder and slower work but the results are lasting.

The truth simply is, as the Winston Churchill quote says: whether we agree or not, whether we like it or not, and whether it fits our beliefs and perceptions or not, it makes life a lot easier when we let go of illusion, avoidance and denial and become aligned with the truth. The path to doing this is to acknowledge our beliefs and perceptions as simply that. As we do this, and replace them for more helpful beliefs and perceptions, it becomes clear that all these are simply choices and not necessarily truth. So, we become less attached to certain ways of being and views of reality. We become adaptable and more open to seeing different points of view, open to accepting the truth when it presents. In the meantime, where we do have beliefs, it makes sense to choose only those beliefs that help us move forward, and create more joy and love.

Chapter 14

Self-esteem and self-acceptance

Individuality is only possible if it unfolds from wholeness.
David Bohm

As I started to work with more and more people, I started to see that self-esteem and self-acceptance were intrinsic to people's well-being and their ability to move through their issues. A good self-esteem is all about accepting the self. It is not necessary to like every aspect of yourself before you can accept yourself. The starting point here is acceptance. To accept yourself fully and completely, exactly as you are with all the bits you don't like or feel aren't good enough. When these bits are not accepted it does not make them go away, they just become hidden and act like a festering sore hindering the development of a good and healthy self-esteem. The very hiddenness of them makes them feel sinister and wrong and confirms that, at heart, we are unlikeable or defective in some way. Acceptance of all the bits we don't like, physical, emotional, mental and spiritual, of all the places where we feel not good enough, fraudulent and ugly, will then allow us the opportunity to look at all these bits in the light, see them for what they are, let go of some and work on that which we choose to. Much of what we don't like will be unimportant—a fat stomach, knobbly knees or a big nose. Other things will show themselves as opportunities for growth. Perhaps a noticing of how we are easily triggered into anger and a motivation to become less so, for example. Other things may be insecurities we have which we will be able to let go of once we have had the courage to accept them and really look into them.

It is up to each person to build up their own self-esteem foundations and we can only do this well when we have control over the building materials, a good understanding of what is there already in our foundations that may need replacing or removing. It is this knowledge that needs to be imparted to clients. That they are in charge of the building of themselves, and that a low sense of self-worth is not something that they have no control over. It is important to look into where they have bought into the low self-esteem and release those judgments.

From early childhood we start to get a sense of ourselves from others' reflections. We learn what is good and bad from others and how to behave in order to be able to fit in and function in society. Sometimes this teaching is not ideal and may teach us that there is something wrong with us, especially when it is done with criticism or disapproval; children can internalize this and start to feel defective or not good enough. They then strive to get approval by changing and behaving in a way that gains approval. This desire for approval and acceptance is evolutionarily appropriate and aids in our survival as children and in our flourishing as we grow. However, there comes a time when we need to make sure our foundations rest on our own internal sense of ourselves and our own self-acceptance and self-love, rather than the approval or disapproval that can be given and withdrawn by others. Relying on others for acceptance and self-esteem is a precarious position, it means that our sense of self-worth rises and falls with the moods and opinions of others. This means that the 'other' that is looked to for approval then creates who we are and how we act. We suppress that which is not seen as acceptable and encourage that which others like. When we look at everything that we don't like or have suppressed about ourselves, we may see parts that are really worthwhile and useful, characteristics that others have judged. For example, you may find that you have a strong will which was criticized as stubbornness by others, or a kind and compassionate heart that was ridiculed as being 'soft' and weak. It is necessary to dismantle the old masks and facades that have been put in place and look at the truth of it all, and build from there.

We rest ourselves on four pillars of self-esteem: worthiness, self-determination, uniqueness and belonging. If any of these pillars are shaky, cracked or weak we start to see symptoms form, such as anxiety, self-destructive patterns and depression. This initially became obvious to me through working with adolescents, I was able to also recognize it in adult clients who are more able to hide it or compensate.

It's not that we have to feel good about ourselves all the time because, god knows, that seems an enormous leap for most of us, and why anyway? What's the point? It seems to me that if we all had this kind of self-esteem we would believe we had made it—no place else to go, nothing to learn and no areas of improvement to work on. What would we do with the rest of our lives? We seem to have set up an idea in popular culture that self-esteem is all about thinking we are fabulous all the time, even to the point of unreality. People say positive affirmations every day as though these have some miraculous power to fix us and make us different. Of course this invariably leads to disappointment, the realization that I'm still just me with all my weird and unlikeable bits still intact!

The belief that self-esteem is about always thinking you are fantastic is unfortunate. Ironically, it sets us up to fail. We think that if I don't think I'm wonderful all the time then my self-esteem isn't good enough and therefore I'm not good enough. Self-esteem is really more of an unshakable core, knowing that I am okay, that I belong, that I am worthy, that I am self-determining and that I am unique. With this at the core we are able to withstand the regular assaults we, and others, make on ourselves. We can recognize that we have done the wrong thing, made the wrong decision, have done something unlikeable, but it does not define who we are or make us intrinsically unworthy. So, we can hold positive self-worth and still feel bad about ourselves and what we have done.

If on the other hand we decide that we have to feel a certain way, i.e., good about ourselves to have good self-esteem, then we can never feel regret or concern about something we have done. This means we can never make mistakes or do the wrong thing without losing our sense of self-worth. A lot of time and energy can be wasted fighting this 'wrong' feeling, resulting in denial of our real feelings and the attempted replacement with feelings we believe are more acceptable. Due to this kind of determined denial we can, over time, completely lose touch with how we feel and even believe our own propaganda, that we are finally feeling the right feeling. This feels okay for a while, but is an incredibly shaky foundation and destined to collapse, as the basis for it is the opposite of self-worth; it is in fact a deep sense of not being good enough to such an extent that I have to hide it even from myself.

How different it is to simply accept how we feel. It doesn't have to mean anything about us, except that it is how we are feeling right now. It doesn't have to have a story or even a reason. It simply is, and is neither bad nor good. We don't judge it and the feeling moves along. It doesn't have to become part of our identity, losing the judgment helps us move from feeling to feeling to learn as we go. Just feelings. This then does not become bound up in how we feel about ourselves, and we don't have to compare this feeling to the one we 'should' be having. According to...?

Self-esteem is not magical or complicated or even about totting up all our good points and ignoring the bits we don't like, these bits are in fact where we could grow and present wonderful opportunities for us. Self-esteem is our foundation. It is where we live, where we come from in all we do and it is the knowing that despite all the parts that need work, bits we don't like and challenges we face, we can manage. It is a feeling of "I am enough." When we have this feeling we have the courage to uncover parts of ourselves that have been hidden from the light, to explore where our foundations may be a bit shaky and need work, so we can continue to grow and build on them and know we won't collapse.

The four pillars of self-esteem

There are four pillars that make up our foundations.

Worthiness

Worthiness is about feeling that you are enough. That you are worthy of taking on challenges, of growing and learning, of setting boundaries and of allowing your heart to be your own guide. That you are worthy of giving and receiving love, worthy to take up space on the planet. To be worthy requires trust in yourself and your own knowing and a recognition that you have a purpose, unique attributes and skills and that the world would not be the same without you.

Where do you feel that you are not worthy? How about charging clients? Is this an uncomfortable process? Why? What feelings come up for you? How about boundary setting? What happens to you when clients have very strong expectations about what you will do for them and what they want you to do. Are you able to be your best at work? What stops you? Where do you feel you have to change who you are in order to gain approval?

Belonging

Belonging is a feeling of oneness with all that is. It is a sense that you fit, that you are where you are supposed to be, doing what you are supposed to do and that you are doing your best. Belonging is knowing you can do it and that you are able. It is also an acknowledgement of the unity of all people and the idea that you have a sense of purpose, a place in the universe. You are not a mistake or an accident.

Where do you feel like a fraud? Where do you feel you have to change who you are in order to be accepted? Where do you feel you belong? Where do you feel you don't belong? How do these feelings of not belonging get in the way? How is fitting in different to belonging?

Uniqueness

Uniqueness complements belonging and reminds us that we do not have to be the same as everyone else to belong. It tells us we all have our own unique purpose, skill sets and abilities to achieve that purpose. It is about who we are uniquely, what makes you you. It is where we fit in the world, where we belong as part of the plan, in all of our uniqueness and purpose.

Where do you feel you may have stifled your uniqueness to fit in? What are some of your unique points? Take a few moments to feel what your purpose might be and how you may be uniquely equipped for it.

Self-determination

Self-determination is the final pillar. It is about how we use our uniqueness and worthiness to make our own decisions. To be able to decide for ourselves, right or wrong, and receive the learning from that. It is how we dance to the beat of our own drum, run our own race, and thus are able to take full responsibility for our lives, our development and growth. Self-determination makes us accountable for what we do and allows us to take full advantage of the opportunity we have to learn and grow through experience, and through our own choices.

Where do you feel restricted in following your heart? Who or what restricts you? Where are you able to follow your own path? How does it feel when you do that?

Spending time pondering these questions is useful in determining which of your foundations are shaky and in what way. This idea is also a very useful tool with clients to help them explore what holds them back, and to explore beliefs they may have about themselves.

It is important as practitioners working with others that we have worked on these foundations ourselves, and revisit them to check how they are going and where they may have become shaky. If we become practiced at doing this, it makes it much easier to lead clients through this discovery process of what their foundations are, and what would be useful to work on for them. All of us have self-esteem challenges at some time, but if you work on these foundations you become aware of where you are weak and have a chance to strengthen these. This is of prime importance for clients, as without adequate self-esteem their development and growth, and their ability to take on challenges and withstand rough times is extremely limited. When they have these strengthened they have the freedom to take risks and even fail, and yet not lose their sense of self-worth.

As we all grow and learn and build upon these foundations into the people we want to be, and as we strive to meet our potential, it is important to revisit these basic foundations regularly as they continue to provide our strength and stability; as we grow taller and bigger, the foundations may need to be increasingly strengthened.

Chapter 15

Where to from here? An invitation to the new paradigm

Connecting oneself to the growth and development of the species can provide enormous meaning... for the practitioner.
Skuvholt

When we look at human well-being it is clear that scientific advances have in a great many ways increased the physical comfort and health of humans. Our well-being, though, is not simply about physical wellness and comfort. We still see daily those that have all the physical comforts that they need and want, yet they are still suffering from unhappiness, loneliness, depression, grief, fear or anxiety. It is obvious, then, that science in its current form can only go so far in alleviating the suffering or increasing the well-being of humankind. If we are interested in helping and healing, then we must also address the spiritual, that which is beyond the physical. It is important to talk about and work with the psycho-spiritual qualities previously mentioned in this book, to address values, connection, love and hope within our work with people as well as those things that can be scientifically validated.

I am full of hope for the end of the polarization between science and spirituality and can see that over the past couple of decades these two ways of seeing the world have come closer. They are both of great importance for the development and growth of humanity, to see the dialogue forming between the two is wonderful.

Science is a wonderful world of discovery and experimentation. Science prizes the mind and what can be created or understood from science regardless of the repercussions of the creation. Scientific progress lurches along like a small child who has not reached the developmental stage of being able to evaluate consequences and think in terms of ethics. Ethics are only applied after the discoveries are made when it is often too late. The Dalai Lama says in his book *The universe in a single atom* that there is, " a general assumption that ethics are relevant only to the application of science and not the actual pursuit of science," and that, "the scientist as an individual and the community of scientists in general occupy a morally neutral position with no responsibility for the fruits they have discovered."

A more 'spiritual' approach, and by this I simply mean, one where the guiding aim is altruistic and compassionate, taking into account all the repercussions to all who inhabit the earth, would help to moderate scientific progress, to shape it so that it best meets the needs of the development and growth of humans, not materially anymore, but spiritually; that the discoveries of science are aimed at the highest good for all. Compassion, love, altruism and hope as well as, of course, ethics are the guiding light into the future of science, and, yes these can go together.

A spiritual approach to science, and here I do not mean religion, but a basic respect for the dignity of all living things would help science humanize itself. Science needs to keep a basic altruistic direction or else it is rudderless, and can be used for unethical ends.

Simply believing in an objective world, in which nothing can be known except through science, is like believing that the Bible is literally true, and that there is nothing more beyond that. Science is one amazing and continually growing field where we can gain a huge amount of knowing, but it is not the only knowing we have. We must regain the ability to trust our own knowing without necessarily needing proof. Sometimes science can lag behind in its ability to test and prove. We need to gain respect for our own inner wisdom and intuition in order to gain a balance in our pursuit of knowledge and our understanding of the world around us. We know that there are limits to any science. We also know that limiting ourselves to that which can be proven beyond all doubt loses the knowledge of the complexity of the word we live in. Trust yourself and your experience, wisdom and intuition, and put those in the mix with all you know. You will see how this changes things and your own knowing, which comes from the heart bringing the heart back into your practice.

Psychology is coming of age. I remember studying psychology in the early nineties and even then noticing its insecurity, its lack of a proud identity. It seemed that most of my lecturers, and the psychology department itself were desperately trying to get rid of the pseudo science label. They tried to be as scientific as possible and distanced themselves as much as possible from anything they considered unscientific. Freud was taught, important as he is in the history of psychology, but they seemed a little ashamed of him. Jung was considered esoteric and not relevant, and it seemed to me throughout my undergraduate studies that psychology was all about labs and rats and the scientific method. We learnt a lot about the brain, statistics and mental pathology and diagnosis, something about the mind and social psychology, and nothing at all about spirituality, energy or coming from the heart. Nothing about spirituality! Spirituality has been an important part of humanness since humanity existed and yet no discussion or exploration of this. The holy grail of counseling was evidence based therapy, which at that time was CBT. All in all there didn't seem to be a lot of heart in it. Since then, though, a lot has changed. Many new ideas have been introduced into psychological discourse, widening its scope and making room for new and sometimes even old ideas. Some of these new ideas have entered psychology and been embraced so enthusiastically that they have become mainstream. Spirituality has entered into the discourse and there is increasing fraternity between scientists and spiritualists. Witness the Dalai Lama and his collaboration with many leading scientists, resulting in the co-authoring of many books with them, ongoing dialogues and mutual respect. We now have respected scientists talking about energetic interactions between people, empathy, compassion and gratitude. They have found ways to measure these qualities and measure the benefit they may have in improving quality of life and happiness.

There is much that science to date has not been able to measure or to take into account. It is important not to discount these things simply because we have no way of measuring them yet. There is an unspoken general idea that if it cannot be scientifically proven then it cannot exist. Science is moving ahead in great leaps and bounds, and yet much of the time coming back to old, even ancient, wisdom and ideas. It is important we do not throw out the baby with the bathwater.

There is research being conducted about mirror neurons and the idea that perhaps we, as humans, are 'wired' for empathy (Iacoboni/Galleses); there is much discussion and research about the benefits of stilling the mind, in meditation in particular, and mindfulness meditation has now become "evidence-based."

At a conference I recently attended, B. Alan Wallace, a Buddhist scholar, discussed the Buddhist idea of entanglement with a quantum physicist. Recently, quantum physicists have 'discovered' what Buddhism has known for thousands of years as 'entanglement.' This is the knowledge that everything affects everything else. For scientists, it is the discovery that the act of observation on a particle changes how that particle behaves. For Buddhists, it is about mutual interdependence. There is an energy interaction between people. No one is independent and any idea that we are is a fundamental delusion, one that causes suffering and unhappiness and cuts us off from compassion and love. We are all affected by others and it is important to be aware of this as we work with people.

This fits with what we notice about the effects of lack of connection on people's lives, but it is more complicated than simple loneliness. It is about feeling the delusion of separation, a delusion we have already discussed. Scientists have now discovered that this ancient idea of entanglement happens in the micro world (quantum physics) and also in photosynthesis. While a discussion of this is beyond the scope of this book, there is now a scientific basis for discussion on the interdependence of everything, and a scientifically valid reason for exploration into the human experience of this.

Major changes have taken place recently in our understanding of psychology and how people become happy or are able to learn, grow and meet their potential. There is great interest in the new wave of therapies and philosophies in psychology. Positive Psychology focuses on the interconnectedness of people and the building of positive relationships, it encourages engagement, meaning and purpose through the application of strengths-based ideas and gratitude, appreciation, hope and optimism. Mindfulness and ACT have changed the face of how we deal with, and how we see, states such as depression, anxiety and chronic pain; Narrative Therapy honors the experience of the client and focuses on collaborative work and the non-expert approach. All these types of therapies have paved the way for a transition for psychologists to acknowledge the importance of the heart in psychology and to start doing so in love, joy and optimism. This is a whole new way of doing things which we are now ready for as science has taken us full circle and those fluffy un-measurable things that were feelings are now able to be quantified and measured, just as we thought, they are of intrinsic importance in the understanding of human behavior, and human wholeness.

Now is the time to start making changes. There is so much possibility for the focus of our work as psychologists to be less about diagnosing illnesses and finding new ones, and more about facilitating wholeness in people and helping to create more love, joy, compassion and hope in the world. We know that happiness is about gratitude, connectedness and love, and surely we are the ones who can use this knowledge in the service of humanity to create a world where we can meet our potential, and that this aim of clarity and being our best is shared by all. Now is the paradigm change, a transformation of psychology, to make it a way to encourage health and nurture it rather than fix disease. This is the way to transform how we work with others and to expand how we see our role. The highest calling we can have is to be of service, all of us have been called to that or we would not have chosen this as a career. It's now time to get out of our own way and to hold a vision of what we want our service to be.

What if we saw life as a school, a place of opportunities, a place where you can't fail? A place to further our own spiritual growth, full of opportunities to learn? Commonly people tend more to see life as getting in the way. We find a safe place, get a job, a place to live, a safe bolthole to escape from life. When events occur that make us uncomfortable we try to avoid them, deny them, make them all better. It's like life is happening to us against our will. Imagine embracing it all for the opportunities life represents and having the attitude of wonder, "I wonder what I can learn from this?" What a difference that would make, not just in our participation in life but also, importantly, in how much we get out of it, how much we make use of being here on earth.

Our job is the nurturing of human development. This is the most privileged role I can think of, and I wouldn't do any other job. For me this possibility holds all the meaning I need. It is of the utmost importance that we maintain our own psychological clarity and levels of awareness in order to be able to discharge this duty to the best of our ability. Energy follows thought. We nurture and encourage health rather than focus on disease and difficulty.

Love, respect, hope, compassion and non-judgment are key

to being able to create lasting change in ourselves, facilitate it in others and so bring about change to our world. What change? My choice would be a world in which spiritual mastery was the goal of most, and as more and more of us make this choice we affect others so that it becomes easier and easier for them to choose this path until it simply becomes the obvious choice.

New Paradigm Psychology

Epilogue

This has been a huge journey for me. Doubt has accompanied some of my work and growth, the feeling that I need to stay small, who am I to think better of, or even simply add to, some of what I have been taught? What allowed me to work through all this fear and doubt was simply following my heart. There is a sense of such rightness to coming from the heart, and a truth in coming from a place of unconditional love and compassion. All those who are reading this book come from a place of wanting to be of service. In all our training and education it is easy to lose sight of this as the prime driver for what we do. Our egos get involved in the process and we wonder whether we will be good psychologists, whether we will be successful. When we give into this kind of fear and doubt, and start to wonder about our own credibility, then the therapy we offer becomes mostly about our own performance and ability, our toolbox of tricks and techniques, rather than about our client in that moment and how to best be of service to them. I do not suggest here that we get rid of our tools and techniques, they are of great use, there is much research behind them and they have added to the richness of what we can offer to the world as a profession. It is simply about using them appropriately, not as a one-size-fits-all approach. My journey through this has been, as Skuvholt uses the analogy, going from a crude map and formulaic type of therapy, to no map at all. Just simply feeling my way through the therapy hour with the purest intention of being of service. Yes I feel anxious at times, I worry that therapy is not effective for some of my clients, that perhaps they are not getting anything out of it, at times I may not be able to hold this intention steady, and fall into doubt. But I have learned to absolutely do my best, and then say no to doubt. I have discussed perceptions in this book, and they apply also to therapy. All perceptions are simply beliefs and as therapists we are as prone to them as our clients. We will often make assumptions about how our clients are going in therapy and what they are getting out of it. Yalom, A psychotherapist whom I very much admire, has a book dedicated to this idea called *Every Day Gets a Little Closer: A Twice Told Therapy* which addresses the difference in our experience of therapy with a certain client and their experience. Our assumptions are usually unhelpful. They may either make us doubtful about our ability, lose hope, and then not be able to be of service to the client, or they may lead us to be grandiose and expert, losing sight of the client in all our cleverness and expertness.

I have applied all these ideas in my own practice and in my life, not perfectly, but with hope and determination. When I doubt myself, I remember that it is not about me, the question is simply, "How may I be of service?" This question is the most grounding and most helpful I can ever ask. It reminds me of my purpose and of what I am doing. It also highlights that none of this is about me. Because it is not about me, it means that I do not take anything personally. It is simply about the service and what I can offer to make the world a better place. I think this way of being and practicing can change our world, open up new possibilities of hope and compassion. We can be so much more than what we are! There is always more to be and further to go. We have so much potential, both as humans and healers, let's harness it.

This book is for counselors and therapists who are already in practice and as such it does not teach counseling skills. It is about more than simply what we do with clients, but how we 'be' with them, and what else we provide in the service of their highest good. The skills discussed here go far deeper than simply counseling strategies, though these are certainly also important. This book is for people who are looking for more in their practice. A satisfaction of the desire to serve without feeling depleted, an understanding of energy interchange and a discussion of the importance of love, compassion, acceptance, hope and other psycho-spiritual qualities. It is about counseling on the being rather than the doing, and it is for those therapists who are willing live the truth of who they are, and to walk the talk of what they teach and show their clients. It is not an easy path, but there is such joy and satisfaction in it that it is impossible to imagine going back to the old.

This book is about the practice of coming from the heart. It is about full integration of ourselves in our service to others. It is about 'being' a counselor, not 'doing' a counselor. This means that we must always be in full alignment with how we are working with others, what we are teaching and in which direction we are leading. Like it or not we are leaders. I speak a lot about the responsibility of the client and their choice, of what they get out of therapy and where they go with it. It is true that only they can make the choice to let go of the past, to live in the moment, to be responsible for their energetic output and actions. However, this does not mean we have no function and no responsibility. We must live the truth of what we say and what we teach so that others can follow a path we have already trodden, so we can be helpful as they encounter snags and difficulties on this path. We may feel that with all our study and all our work on ourselves we have done enough, but the work is never done, we must remain fully aware and open to our next step forward in our own growth and development. How could we possibly encourage others to let go of old patterns, leave their comfort zones and step into the new if we are unable and unwilling to do this ourselves in every moment. This choice of profession carries responsibilities as well as privileges and we must be willing to shoulder these in order to truly be of service.

Let the ideas in this book sit with you for a while, try them on and see how they fit with your practice and what they may offer to you and your clients. It is my hope they can be of service to you and those you work with.

Appendix

List of examples of Psycho-Spiritual qualities

Unconditional love
Compassion
Sense of humor
Equanimity
Calm assurance
Wisdom
Kindness
Mercy
Justice
Courage
Trust
Hope
Faith
Honor
Honesty
Generosity
Gratitude
Acceptance
Strength
Joy

Benevolence
Receptivity
Nurturance
Resilience
Self-acceptance
Worthiness
Self-determination
Optimism
Innocence
Patience
Serenity
Clarity
Wonder
Adaptability
Creativity
Humility
Appreciation
Loyalty
Awareness
Contentment

**PSYCHE
BOOKS**

PSYCHE BOOKS

PSYCHOLOGY

Psyche Books cover all aspects of psychology and matters relating to the head.
The study of the mind - interactions, behaviors, functions; developing and expanding our understanding of self.
Psychology: All forms, all disciplines including business, criminal, educational, sport. Therapies: clinical analysis, CBT, counselling, hypnosis, NLP, psychoanalysis, psychodrama, psychotherapy, role-play.
Archetypes, behavioral science, CAM therapies, experimental work, popular psychology, psychological studies, neuroscience.
Including but not restricted to: Behavior, brain games, personality, mental health, mind coaching, nature of the mind, treatment strategies, unconscious mind.
If you have enjoyed this book, why not tell other readers by posting a review on your preferred book site.

Recent bestsellers from PSYCHE BOOKS are:

The Chi of Change
How Hypnotherapy Can Help You Heal and Turn Your Life
Around - Regardless of Your Past
Peter Field
A ground breaking book that will change forever the way you
think about your feelings and emotions!
Paperback: 978-1-78279-351-9 ebook: 978-1-78279-350-2

Emotional Life - Managing Your Feelings to Make the
Most of Your Precious Time on Earth
How to Gain Mastery Over Your Feelings
Doreen Davy
Emotional Life explains how we can harness our own emotional
power in order to live happier, healthier and more fulfilling lives.
Paperback: 978-1-78279-276-5 ebook: 978-1-78279-275-8

Creating Trance and Hypnosis Scripts
Gemma Bailey
A well-known hypnotherapist reveals her secret tips on how to
help others quit smoking, lose weight and beat the blues.
Paperback: 978-1-84694-197-9

Depression: Understanding the Black Dog
Stephanie June Sorrell
This accessible work addresses a universal health issue with a
toolbag yielding the ways depression manifests and insight into
the treatments available.
Paperback: 978-1-78279-165-2 ebook: 978-1-78279-174-4

Smashing Depression
Escaping the Prison and Finding a Life
Terence Watts
Depression is an insidious enemy, gradually eroding confidence
and willpower... but this book restores the spirit and strength to
fight back - and win!
Paperback: 978-1-78279-619-0 ebook: 978-1-78279-618-3

Why Men Like Straight Lines and Women Like Polka Dots
Gender and Visual Psychology
Gloria Moss
Discover how men and women perceive the world differently and
why they won't agree on the colour or shape of the sofa!
Paperback: 978-1-84694-857-2 ebook: 978-1-84694-708-7

Head versus Heart
Michael Hampson
The most important new material on the enneagram in thirty years,
Head Versus Heart questions how we engage with the world around
us.
Paperback: 978-1-90381-692-9

Mastering Your Self, Mastering Your World
Living by the Serenity Prayer
John William Reich
Mastery over the events of our life is key to our well-being; this
book explains how to achieve that mastery.
Paperback: 978-1-78279-727-2 ebook: 978-1-78279-726-5

The Secret Life of Love and Sex
Making Relationships Work and What to Do If They Don't
Terence Watts
Men and women think differently and 'work' differently - but they
don't know that! SO sometimes a white lie or a secret is a good
thing...
Paperback: 978-1-78279-464-6 ebook: 978-1-78279-463-9

Powerful Mind Through Self-Hypnosis
A Practical Guide to Complete Self-Mastery
Cathal O'Briain
Powerful Mind Through Self-Hypnosis is the definitive book, teaching
self-hypnosis as a pure and natural form of self-healing.
Paperback: 978-1-84694-298-3 ebook: 978-1-78099-761-2

Readers of ebooks can buy or view any of these bestsellers by
clicking on the live link in the title. Most titles are published in
paperback and as an ebook. Paperbacks are available in traditional
bookshops. Both print and ebook formats are available online.

Find more titles and sign up to our readers' newsletter at
http://www.johnhuntpublishing.com/mind-body-spirit.
Follow us on Facebook at https://www.facebook.com/OBooks and
Twitter at https://twitter.com/obooks.